Society **T**oday

SHUTDOWN

The Anatomy of a Shipyard Closure

John Withington was born in Manchester in 1947 and was educated at Manchester Grammar School and New College, Oxford, where he read Modern History.

He was a producer with BBC Radio, then industrial correspondent for ATV in Birmingham. Subsequently he was a reporter on various Thames Television programmes including the network current affairs programme, 'TV Eye'. He is the producer/director of the Thames Television documentaries 'Shutdown', to which this book is related.

He has contributed to 'Channel Four News' and 'The Business Programme', and has written for a variety of newspapers and publications, including the *Guardian*, the *Observer*, the *Daily Express*, *New Society*, the *New Statesman*, *Campaign* and *Marketing Week*.

SHUTDOWN

The Anatomy of a Shipyard Closure

John Withington

Statistical analysis by
Sue Straughair, Shamalah Tucker and Peter Wybrow

Bedford Square Press

Published by
BEDFORD SQUARE PRESS of the
National Council for Voluntary Organisations
26 Bedford Square, London WC1B 3HU

First published 1989
Copyright © John Withington, 1989

Typeset by AKM Associates (UK) Ltd, Southall, London
Printed and bound in England by
J.W. Arrowsmith Limited, Bristol

British Library Cataloguing in Publication Data
Withington, John
  Shutdown: the anatomy of a shipyard
  closure — (Society today)
  1. Cleveland. South Bank. Shipbuilding
  industries. Personnel. Redundancy.
  Social aspects
  I. Title   II. Series
  306'.36

ISBN 0-7199-1230-X

Contents

Acknowledgements

I should like to take the opportunity to thank Peter Wybrow and, in the early stages, Barry Warrington of Teesside Polytechnic for superintending the research. I should like to thank Shamalah Tucker for her work on questionnaire design and analysis, and the tables in this book, and Sue Straughair for her work on questionnaire design, running the fieldwork, and analysing the diaries completed by interviewees. I should like to thank both of them for the invaluable help they gave in responding to the many questions and queries I generated as I wrote the statistical sections of the book. I also offer my gratitude to the team of interviewers for their enthusiasm and dedication.

None of what we did would have been possible without the patience of the 200 interviewees, each of whom answered more than a thousand questions over the life of the project. I am also indebted to the smaller number of people I interviewed in depth for their friendliness and openness, often in adversity. Thanks are also due to the Thames Television researchers, Sam Hanson and Christine Peaker, who worked on the earlier stages of the project, and who helped me crystallise some of the thoughts that appear in this book.

On a more personal level, I should like to thank my son for his tolerance and patience when I retired to my office for long spells of solitary communion with the word processor, and, above all, my wife, for her unfailing encouragement and support.

John Withington
November 1988

Introduction

The most important aim of this book is to give a voice to those who have no voice – to those who, in their millions, have been thrown out of work as Britain's manufacturing industry has contracted during the eighties, and whose plight has all too often been ignored, as those in work have become better off. Nine of them speak at length in these pages about the experiences of being made redundant when their shipyard closed, and of the unemployment that often followed. The experiences of another 200 have been distilled into a statistical picture of the experience.

First, though, a brief account of the origins of the book, and a few words of explanation about its structure. The story begins with an ambitious television project, perhaps the most ambitious ever mounted, on the subject of unemployment. In 1986, I was working at Thames Television, where it was strongly felt that one of the most significant events of the eighties was the return of mass unemployment on a scale unknown since the thirties. It was felt too that television had not done justice to this major event in the nation's history.

It was considered that much of the coverage of unemployment had tended to be anecdotal, and that we must find an approach that preserved the human interest of the anecdotal style – so important in television – but one which also had a firm statistical base. The way to do this would be to take one workplace that was closing, and examine what happened to the people who used to work there. This was to be done by taking a representative sample of the workforce, and conducting regular interviews with them over a long period following the closure. It was felt that we should choose a manufacturing site – it was, after all, the shakeout in manufacturing that was responsible for almost all of the rise in unemployment during the first half of the eighties.

While this thought process was going on, the closure was suddenly announced in May 1986 of Smith's Dock, a shipyard at South Bank, on the outskirts of Middlesbrough. Smith's Dock seemed the ideal case study for a number of reasons. It had a big enough workforce, more than 1,400, to enable the study sample to be of sufficient size. It was situated in one of the areas of the country that had been worst hit by unemployment, and, in many ways, it was a classic 1980s closure. The victim was in an industry, like so many others, in which Britain had once led the world, but in which we now found it impossible to compete with other countries.

Following the choice of Smith's Dock, it seemed natural to contract the local polytechnic, Teesside Polytechnic in Middlesbrough, to do the research. It was at this point, in August 1986, that I was asked to make the programme. My brief was to produce a 'historical document' about unemployment. We had to move quickly, because people were already leaving the yard. The first had begun to drift away as soon as the closure was announced, and the first compulsory redundancies were to be at the beginning of October.

Quickly, I put together a brief of what we wanted to find out. What steps had people taken to find new jobs? If they had been successful, how did their new jobs compare with the jobs they had lost at Smith's Dock? Had they been able to get jobs locally, or had they had to move? How much help and advice were they given? Had they been offered any re-training?

For those who did not find work, we wanted to know what effect this had on the family finances and on family relationships. What was the effect on their health and morale? How did the unemployed fill their days? How satisfied were they with the services they were offered from the benefits authorities and the job centres? Did they become involved with the Black Economy?

In order to provide us with answers, the Polytechnic selected a random sample of 200 of the workforce, chosen to be representative in terms of the distribution of the various trades within the yard. We decided to interview them 10 times over the next two years. The Polytechnic recruited a team of 11 interviewers. The first questionnaire was drawn up, and interviewing began just before Christmas 1986. (There is a more detailed note on the research methods in the appendix.)

Schedule of interviews

Round 1 December 1986 – January 1987
Round 2 February 1987 – March 1987
Round 3 April 1987 – May 1987
Round 4 July 1987 – August 1987
Round 5 October 1987 – November 1987
Round 6 December 1987 – January 1988
Round 7 April 1988 – May 1988
Round 8 June 1988 – July 1988
Round 9 September 1988 – October 1988
Round 10 November 1988 – December 1988

In February 1988, a year after the final closure of the yard, material gathered from Rounds 1 to 6 was used as the basis of a Thames Television documentary, 'Shutdown', which was transmitted on the ITV network. The statistics from the survey were allied with vivid accounts of the experience of unemployment taken from filmed interviews with those who had lost their jobs. A second documentary, covering events in the second year after the closure, was scheduled for transmission in April 1989.

Two television documentaries, with a combined running length of two hours, cannot hope to include more than a flavour of the formidable body of data amassed by the Polytechnic. Nor can they hope to include all the fascinating details about life after redundancy, revealed in the many interviews that I did with individuals over long periods of time. Repairing those omissions is another purpose of this book.

Like the documentaries, it is based on two things: the statistical findings from the Polytechnic's research, illustrated by case studies from my interviews with a small selection of the forty or fifty former Smith's Dock workers to whom I have spoken at considerable length. The case studies are told almost entirely in the subjects' own words. Where the subject has had a spouse or partner, their account of the experience of redundancy has been treated as being of as much importance as the experience of the person actually made redundant. Most of the case studies are wide-ranging in subject matter. Though I have tried to put each one together with the research findings that seem most relevant, there is a great deal in each one that is also pertinent to other sections. So while in Barry Reed's case history in chapter 4, for example, you will find much that is relevant to 'Looking for Work', you will also find a lot that strikes a chord in 'On the Dole' or 'Filling in the Day'.

Some, but not all, of the people featured in the case studies were also featured in the television programme, and some, but not all, were also included in the Polytechnic's sample of 200. The case studies are not based on information given to the Polytechnic's interviewers, which was provided in confidence, and for the purpose of statistical analysis, on the understanding that no information would be identified with a particular individual. They are based on information and opinions given to me in the knowledge that they might be used for transmission or publication.

The book is not an examination of whether it was right or wrong to close Smith's Dock. However, the first chapter sets out the background to the story in terms of the overall problems of the area surrounding Smith's Dock, and the overall problems facing ship-building, and the second tells the story of the events leading up to the closure. All of these factors, of course, played their part in influencing people's reaction to redundancy. The third chapter gives a brief 'profile' of the workforce, and, at the end of the book, I have tried to make an assessment of the overall costs and benefits, if any, of the closure to those involved.

Did redundancy prove to be a blessing for some – opening their eyes to new opportunities, allowing them more leisure and more time with their friends and families, providing them with a cash payment that they were able to use to pay off debts or improve their homes? Or were these benefits outweighed by the demoralising effects of being thrown out of work in one of the most depressed labour markets in the industrialised world?

Finally, there is a brief postscript which updates the story to the end of 1988. It tells briefly what happened to the individuals featured in the case histories, and what happened to the area and local economy as a whole. It also includes the findings from the Polytechnic's later interviews.

There are a couple of technical points about the statistics. The first is that the sample changed in size during the survey, with some interviewees dropping out, and others being recruited to replace them. At all times, the percentages I quote are percentages of the number of people in the survey at the particular time. Secondly, as will become clear, the 'unemployed' were not a static group. There were continual movements in and out of work. The 'unemployed' or those 'in work' referred to throughout the book are not always, therefore, made up of the same people.

CHAPTER 1

TOP OF THE UNEMPLOYMENT LEAGUE

*In Cleveland, we're top of the
unemployment league, aren't we?*
(Unemployed plater)

The closure of a workplace has been one of the most common economic experiences in Britain over the last decade. It has been undergone in thousands of British factories by millions of British workers. Unemployment rose steadily from the mid-seventies, until by January 1986, six and a half years after Mrs Thatcher came to power, it had reached a peak of more than three and a quarter million. Critics of the Government pointed out that it would have been even higher, but for a series of changes in the way the figure was calculated, almost all of which had the effect of reducing it.

Five years before the national figure reached its peak, the county of Cleveland had gone to the top of the unemployment league, as the county with the highest jobless rate in mainland Britain. It was one of Cleveland's few claims to fame. Hacked out of what had once been the North Riding of Yorkshire, and joined to bits of County Durham, it was the successor to the County Borough of Teesside, which itself had had an existence of only six years. No wonder its very whereabouts were something of a mystery to strangers.

In fact, Cleveland is a combination of heavy industrial areas and rather attractive hills and countryside on either side of the River Tees; the main towns being Middlesbrough, Stockton and Hartlepool. The industry first arrived in the nineteenth century. As the industrial revolution brought upheaval throughout Britain, nowhere changed more dramatically than Cleveland.

In 1825, it established its place in world economic history with the opening of the Stockton and Darlington Railway, the first steam-powered public railway in the world. Middlesbrough at that time was a hamlet of just 25 inhabitants. By 1914, its population had soared to 120,000. It was the fastest-growing town in Victorian England. Gladstone, on a visit in 1862, described it as 'the youngest child of England's enterprise . . . an infant, but an infant Hercules'.

Middlesbrough's explosive growth had begun in 1830, when six Quakers bought up 500 acres of land in order to found a port on the Tees to handle coal from the Durham Coalfield. They planned a town of 5,000 people. The thing that changed its destiny so dramatically was iron. The first ironworks was founded as early as 1839, but it was the discovery of iron ore in the Cleveland Hills to the south of Middlesbrough in 1850 that transformed it into that infant Hercules.

By 1858, there were 39 blast furnaces on Teesside. By 1870, the area had become the world's leading producer of iron, and remained so for the rest of the century. There was no doubt which industry dominated the local economy. Even the local football team carried the name – Middlesbrough Ironopolis. Metal manufacturing continued to be a pillar of Teesside's economy, with the area later becoming one of the British Steel Corporation's principal sites.

Chemicals arrived rather later. The industry had been established in a rudimentary form on Teesside in the early nineteenth century, but it was when ICI came to Billingham, then a village over the river from Middlesbrough, in the 1920s that this second pillar of Cleveland's prosperity was firmly established. After the Second World War, ICI built a second major plant at Wilton, to the southeast of Middlesbrough.

The other dominant strands in Teesside's industry were mechanical engineering and shipbuilding. There were great names here too, like Dorman Long – once the biggest iron and steel firm in Britain and the builders of the Sydney Harbour Bridge.

The story of shipbuilding was also spectacular. It had appeared at Stockton as far back as the seventeenth century. By the end of the eighteenth century, the Tees was turning out ships for the American War of Independence, then, later, the Napoleonic Wars. By the end of the nineteenth century, with the United Kingdom supplying 82 per cent of the world's shipping needs, Teesside alone was turning out a staggering 15 per cent of all the world's ships. Famous names included William Gray of Hartlepool, one of the largest yards in Britain, and Smith's Dock at South Bank on the outskirts of Middlesbrough. At the industry's peak, there were nine yards on the river.

It was in the thirties that alarm bells first began to ring on Teesside about what was seen as an over-dependence on too few industries and too few large companies. The Great Depression was an awful warning. Times were bad everywhere, but on Teesside they were appalling. Male unemployment ran at twice the national average, and in 1932, it climbed as high as 39 per cent.

Those days seemed far away, though, in the sixties as the era of 'you've never had it so good' melted into the white heat of Harold Wilson's technological revolution. Both were supposed to mean good times for Teesside. First, Lord Hailsham, Harold Macmillan's 'Minister for the North-east' donned a cloth cap, and designated it a growth area. Then Harold Wilson's Government produced a strategic plan that envisaged its becoming 'one of the most productive, efficient, and beautiful regions in Britain'.

This *Teesside Survey and Plan* predicted a dramatic growth in population – an increase of 50 per cent in 20 years, and the creation of 120,000 new jobs. There was to be reclamation of land by the Tees, and an ambitious road-building programme. Incentives were provided to private industry to come and invest in the area. It was recognised, though, that the new jobs would not come from Teesside's traditional industries – steel, chemicals, engineering, and shipbuilding. If anything, because of productivity gains, it was believed that employment in these industries would actually decline. Instead, new industries were supposed to come in, producing consumer goods. The service sector was expected to grow.

These were happy days. In 1965, fewer than 2 per cent of the local labour force were out of work. Even in 1974, the figure had only reached 4 per cent, but then as the first oil crisis plunged the world into recession, Teesside was about to suffer an economic catastrophe. The hopes of the *Survey and Plan* were to be cruelly disappointed. There was some large-scale investment in chemicals, but it did not create new jobs. Steel, instead of finding itself in a phase of ambitious expansion, had to go in for severe retrenchment. As for the new industries, they never came.

Cleveland's heavy dependence on manufacturing now became a severe handicap, as unemployment rose to nearly 10 per cent by the end of the decade. Worse was to come, though. Between 1979 and 1981, it doubled, reaching close to 20 per cent. These were the years when a sixth of British manufacturing industry was literally scrapped.

In 1975, out of a total workforce of 245,000 in Cleveland, 105,000 worked in manufacturing industry. Of them, 56,000, split virtually equally, worked in steel and chemicals, and 18,000 in mechanical engineering and shipbuilding. During the next 11 years, Cleveland lost no fewer than 63,000 jobs – one in every four. That was bad enough, but the decline in manufacturing was even more striking. Fifty thousand jobs, nearly half, were destroyed in the sector that had been the mainstay of its prosperity.

So Cleveland had found its way to the top of the unemployment league. By the middle of 1986, the jobless figure was standing at more than 20 per cent against a national average of under 12, and within that depressing overall picture, there were pockets where the problem was even more serious. Male unemployment for the county was more than 25 per cent, and in Middlesbrough, it was over 27 per cent. There were 28 people on the dole for every vacancy.

If you applied a magnifying glass to the figures, among the black spots, you could pick out spots that were blacker still. The worst place of all was South Bank, home of the Smith's Dock shipyard. Here the overall unemployment rate was more than 37 per cent, and male unemployment was a heart-breaking 45 per cent. Focus in even tighter, and you would find whole streets where virtually no one had a job.

Apart from its sheer size, Teesside's unemployment problem had other peculiarities, like the high proportion of people who were long-term unemployed. More than 40 per cent of the men without work had been unemployed for more than two years, compared with a national average of less than 30 per cent, while in Middlesbrough, the figure reached 45 per cent.

In its frequent pleas for help, Cleveland County Council tried to stress that it was not a typical victim of the 'British Disease' – usually considered to be low investment, outdated equipment, poor productivity and abrasive labour relations. The council argued:

> The problems of Cleveland are not those of the caricature of a depressed area with low productivity, lack of competitiveness, poor industrial relations and a record of low levels of industrial investment . . . Cleveland has a very productive, highly capital intensive, but narrow manufacturing base.

Cleveland had one industry, though, where the problems seen locally were simply a part of a tragedy being played out all over the world. This was shipbuilding. As recently as 40 years ago, Britain was still building more than half the world's ships. Then came the kind of decline that became a common sight in industries in which we had once led the world – cars, steel, motorcycles and so on. As was so often the case, our dominant position was seized by competitors from the Far East. While Britain's share of the world market fell to around

1 per cent, Japan was picking up half of all the orders on offer, with South Korea taking around 15 per cent. This drama was made into a crisis by the world recession that followed the oil crisis of 1974. The bottom was well and truly knocked out of the world shipbuilding market as demand, particularly for large oil tankers, evaporated, and prices tumbled. Soon shipbuilders were not so much competing to sell ships, as competing to give them away.

In the midst of this chaos, Britain's shipbuilding companies were nationalised and, in 1977, British Shipbuilders was born. At the time it was formed, it employed 87,000 workers, but changing the ownership of the business made no difference to its problems. After a brief revival in the early eighties, shipbuilding contract prices went crashing down again. It was not just Britain that was affected. Sweden virtually gave up merchant shipbuilding, and even Japan was looking to reduce the size of its industry by 20 per cent. Japanese workers had to be made redundant.

Countries competed with each other by making ever more special offers – subsidised prices, cheap loans, deferred payments. In 1985, it was estimated that the governments of the shipbuilding nations were spending $5 billion a year subsidising shipbuilding orders, 25 per cent of what the orders brought in. Rules were introduced within the European Community to try to stop its shipbuilding industries from using ever more spectacular giveaways to cut each other's throats.

They prescribed a limit on subsidies of 28 per cent of the contract value, which might seem generous enough, but which British Shipbuilders described as a 'very severe target'. Anyway, the South Koreans, it was claimed, were making even these subsidies look mean. They were said to be offering to build ships at 20 per cent less than the cost of the materials involved.

Still the market obstinately refused to recover. Prices of new ships halved during the first half of the eighties, but with second-hand ship prices falling by 80 per cent, even this was not enough to generate business. This was hardly surprising when you think that very large oil tankers, which a few years before would earn enough to pay for themselves in two or three voyages, now could not generate enough revenue to cover their operating costs.

Global conditions, then, were dreadful. In 1976, world shipbuilding production was 34 million metric tons; a decade later it was only 18 million. Britain's decline, though, was particularly spectacular. In 1950, we sent 1.4 million tonnes down our slipways. By 1987, the figure we achieved was just 84,000 tonnes.

The blame for this could not be laid at the door of the shipbuilding workforce. At one time, the industry had been a byword for rigid demarcation lines and baffling craftsmen's rituals – with analysts making abstruse calculations about how many different tradesmen it took to put in a porthole. By the mid-eighties, though, such restrictive practices were a thing of the past. In 1984, major changes in working conditions in Britain's shipyards had been agreed, and in 1986 and 1987, British Shipbuilders' annual reports praised the workforce for its attitude.

In 1986, it was noted that 'flexibility arrangements agreed with the trade unions [had been] substantially implemented'. The following year, it was noted that 'less than 0.2 per cent of available man-hours was lost through disputes'. Progress of this kind, though, could not provide even the most minimal shelter against the storm raging around the world. People were talking about an upturn in the nineties, and the need to hang on until then, but they had been expecting an upturn for much of the eighties, too.

It was not even clear that British Shipbuilders was in a state to hang on. By the middle of 1986, the workforce was down to just 10,000. Even allowing for the fact that 30,000 now worked in newly privatised warship yards, that was still a far cry from the 87,000 who earned their living from shipbuilding at the time of nationalisation.

Losses had doubled to £137 million. Only 23,000 tonnes of orders had been secured in the previous year, against a target of 200,000, and when the ships actually being worked on were completed, BS's order book would be completely empty. No wonder the new chairman, Philip Hares, warned that without new orders, 'we will all be on the street'. No wonder either that the Tees, which had once supplied 15 per cent of the world's shipping, had gone the way of the rest of the British industry. William Gray's at Hartlepool had closed in 1962, and, when the Haverton Hill shipyard at Stockton closed in 1978, only Smith's Dock at South Bank was left.

The company had a long history, and a reputation for good workmanship. It had arrived at South Bank in 1908, though it is possible to trace back the company's history on Tyneside as far as the eighteenth century. The site at South Bank was marshland, and was under water except at low tide. It had to be reclaimed by using molten slag from a nearby iron works.

At the time when the South Bank yard opened, Smith's Dock was already the biggest ship repairing company in the world. The new site soon employed 3,000 men. In its early years, the yard was known mainly for trawlers and whalers. Then, during the First World War, patrol gunboats built there played a major part in the sea battles against German U-boats.

The shipyard suffered bitterly during the Great Depression, but managed to survive to play a significant role in the Second World War. During its six years, Smith's Dock built more than 70 ships for the Royal Navy. They were mainly 'corvettes', a design based on the whaler. Their speed and manoeuvrability once again put them in the front line in the battle against enemy submarines.

After the war, demand for whalers declined, and Smith's Dock had to develop new markets with tankers and bulk carriers. It also tried to take a slice of the burgeoning North Sea oil and gas industry. In 1966, the yard became the first in Britain to launch a semi-submersible drilling rig. Many other avenues were explored in an effort to follow the twists and turns of world demand, as the yard produced offshore supply and roll on/roll off vessels, container and refrigerated ships.

Smith's Dock, though, could not be insulated any more than any other yard against the icy conditions prevailing in the world market. In 1982, the yard pulled out of ship repairing, shutting down four dry docks. The workforce continued to shrink: 2,200 in 1983, 1,700 in 1984, 1,500 in 1985.

Orders were hard to come by, in spite of the company's worldwide good name, and tireless globe-trotting in search of business by the yard's managing director, Roger Spence, who had spent his whole working life at Smith's Dock. In February 1985, there was relief in the form of an order to build four cargo ships for Cuba. On 13 May 1986, two of those ships – the East Islands and the North Islands – were being built on the slipways at Smith's Dock; the 943rd and 944th vessels in its history.

Now, though, the final chapter of that history was about to be written.

CHAPTER 2

DOOMED

Doomed. On yer bike.
(Graffiti at Smith's Dock)

On 13 May 1986, leaders of the shipbuilding unions had congregated in Newcastle upon Tyne to prepare for a meeting the following day at which British Shipbuilders was due to make its response to their annual pay claim. At least, that is what the unions were expecting.

Those members of the Smith's Dock workforce who tuned in to ITN's 'Channel Four News' that night were informed that their negotiators were going to get a surprise. They also learned something interesting about their shipyard. It was to close. So were two other yards. The workforces at another two were going to be cut. Altogether, 3,500 jobs – representing 30 per cent of the workforce – would be lost. This was what the negotiators were to be told as they tabled their claim.

When the Smith's Dock workers clocked in the following day, some were still stunned, others angry that they should learn the news first on television. Others were sceptical – they had been hearing rumours of closure for years. Any lingering hopes that it was just another rumour, though, were dashed at 3.30 in the afternoon, when the then Secretary of State for Trade and Industry, Paul Channon, asked the Speaker of the House of Commons for permission to make a statement.

MPs were told in a brief preamble that British Shipbuilders had won only one tenth of the orders it needed, that Sweden had pulled out of merchant shipbuilding altogether, that the British Government had invested £1.4 billion in the industry since 1979, and that, yes, Smith's Dock, the Ferguson-Ailsa yard at Troon in Ayrshire, and the Clark Kincaid engine works at Wallsend on the Tyne were to close.

With manpower reductions at two other yards, the loss of jobs would, indeed, be 3,500. The pill was to be sweetened by giving British Shipbuilders £5 million to set up a company known as BSEL – British Shipbuilders Enterprise Limited – to find work for those to be made redundant, and a further £5 million was to be dispensed via various other job-creating agencies.

The Opposition, predictably, were scathing. The Shadow Industry Minister, John Smith, called it 'chilling and desperate news'. As for the money allocated for alleviating its effects, this was dismissed as 'desperate passing of the hat around government departments [that] amounts to no more than putting tiny pieces of sticking plaster over gaping wounds'. Mr Channon's defence of his actions was characterised as a 'wearisome recital of platitudes and ministerial hand-wringing'.

Other Labour members weighed in too. Former Prime Minister James Callaghan said Sweden could do what it liked, but as for Great Britain, 'it is an act of folly for an island . . . to allow its shipbuilding industry to be almost destroyed'.

James Tinn, then the Labour MP for Redcar, the constituency in which Smith's Dock is situated, pointed to its good reputation: 'the first-class work of men and management'. For good measure, he quoted British Shipbuilders themselves: 'Their achievements were confirmed as recently as last November in a letter from Graham Day, the then chairman of British Shipbuilders, in which he discounted rumours of future closures.' Was not the closure announcement 'a shabby return for all their sterling work'?

As for the Secretary of State's measures to soften the blow, Mr Tinn dismissed them as 'little more than a contribution to the funeral expenses of an important sector of the British shipbuilding industry'. Another MP sitting for a shipbuilding constituency, Bob Clay (Sunderland North) asked whether it was not true that 'the whole industry will disappear by the end of this year or early next year'?

On the Conservative side, Teddy Taylor pointed out that the Government's total planned investment in shipbuilding for the next year was only equivalent to four days' subsidy of agriculture. Richard Holt, in whose Langbaurgh constituency many Smith's Dock workers lived, asked whether more financial assistance could be provided, and, particularly, whether there would be help for those who wanted to move to other parts of the country where jobs were more plentiful, but houses were more expensive.

On the whole, though, the Government's supporters rallied around Mr Channon, and he stood by his arguments that orders were not to be had, that shipbuilding's problems were a worldwide, rather than a British phenomenon, that Government support of the industry was as generous as could reasonably be expected, and that the emergency measures announced, to help the men who would be sacked to find new jobs, would be of value.

Outside the House, there were more angry protests. Alex Ferry, General Secretary of the Confederation of Shipbuilding and Engineering Unions, declared: 'British Shipbuilders have killed Middlesbrough. It is a dead town.' For Arthur Seed, a former plater at the yard, the announcement came on his last day of office as mayor of Langbaurgh. To him, it was just another symptom of the North-South divide: 'People south of Birmingham just don't know how much we have suffered already, without another body blow.'

A week after the death sentence was pronounced on Smith's Dock, there was another Parliamentary debate. Paul Channon reiterated the Government's original arguments. This time, though, he got a rougher ride from the Conservative back benches. Richard Holt accused the Government of wringing its hands, and of being ignorant of conditions on Teesside: 'It is time that some members of the Government spent some time living in the North-east, not merely visiting it, in order to understand the impact of their policies on the region.'

Sir Edward du Cann put forward a passionate plea for more Government support for the industry. He pointed to the progress made in industrial relations in the yards: 'British shipyard workers have been steadily putting their house in order and becoming more competitive. There have been huge advances in productivity which is up 15 per cent in the last two years. The absurdities of demarcation are a thing of the past.' He urged the Government to call a halt to the continuing decline, not just of shipbuilding, but of all manufacturing industry:

> Future generations will never forgive us if we do not say that this process of attrition in British manufacturing industry has gone far enough . . . these fine, skilled men who work in the shipyards deserve our support. Once their skills are lost, they will be lost forever.

An Opposition amendment castigating the Government for its 'neglect and indifference' was defeated by 72 votes, but not before there had been another intervention by Smith's Dock's constituency MP, James Tinn. This time, the setting up of BSEL, with its headquarters in Middlesbrough, was dismissed as 'little more than an offer to open up a branch of undertakers to help the bereaved'. As for the Minister's assurance that he supported shipbuilding, that was 'presumably in the same way as a hearse supports the coffin on the way to the grave'.

Mr Tinn spoke with admiration of what he saw as the dedication and resourcefulness of the management of Smith's Dock: 'right up to the time of the closure announcement, an energetic and enterprising management was chasing the few orders that were available.' He spoke too of the social consequences for the area of the closure of the yard, that it would confirm and exacerbate the tendency of Teessiders to become nomads, 'industrial gypsies' as another Labour MP was to put it, in their search for work.

Displaced workers set up businesses and scour the world for work because there is none here at home. There are few construction or industrial sites in the Middle East, for instance, without a sizeable contingent of Teessiders separated from homes and families.

Perhaps his most significant contribution, though, was his analysis of why, in a situation where all shipyards were losing money, Smith's Dock should have been chosen for closure. 'Teesside's reputation for calm and constructive acceptance of industrial decline,' he said, 'has invited only further body blows.' Mr Tinn argued that other areas which had been less 'calm and constructive' had received more sympathetic treatment from the Government, that it was those who caused the most trouble who were most likely to receive consideration.

A similar attitude prevailed in the shipyard itself, where it was noted that yards that had sustained higher losses had been kept going. British Shipbuilders offered different reasons. It argued that, although there had been substantial new investment in Smith's Dock, some of which had barely come on stream when the closure was announced, it lagged behind in other respects. Crucially, it did not have undercover construction facilities. Furthermore, BS was trying to bring all its north-eastern yards together into one company. It had two yards on opposite sides of the river in Sunderland, and the other 30 miles down the road near Middlesbrough. In a situation where someone had to close, there was only one real choice.

Perhaps not surprisingly, few of the Smith's Dock workforce seemed convinced by these arguments. Equally, however, Mr Tinn's analysis that at the end of the day, Teesside shipyard men would submit quietly to their fate seemed to be borne out. There were local protests, and Smith's Dock was well represented in a march to Westminster that coincided with the second Parliamentary debate, but the workforce soon bowed to the inevitable, and concentrated on trying to secure the best possible redundancy terms. All over the yard, the graffiti in paint and chalk proclaimed: 'Doomed!'

Local authorities and trade unions tried to put forward their arguments against closure. Cleveland County Council pointed out that half of the Smith's Dock workforce lived in South Bank, Eston and East Middlesbrough – areas of, even by Cleveland standards, very high unemployment. The effect of the shutdown would be to bring male unemployment in Eston to 34 per cent, in East Middlesbrough to 43 per cent, and in South Bank to 56 per cent. The trade unions argued that the knock-on effect on sub-contractors, suppliers, and even local shops and services meant that another 2,000 jobs would be destroyed in addition to those lost at the yard.

These arguments, however, cut no perceptible ice with the Government, and those putting them forward had no muscle to offer when argument failed, so virtually from the moment the closure was announced, workers began to slip away from the yard. Some went early in the belief that being one of the first to jump might give you a better place in the jobs queue.

To try to help them, British Shipbuilders Enterprise Limited was set to work. This was a company based on two previous models – BSC (Industry) Limited, and NCB (Enterprise) Limited. Their brief had been to provide jobs for steelworkers and miners, respectively, flung out of work when their works or pits closed. Opinions varied as to how successful this strategy had been. Be that as it may, BSEL now had a similar task – to take men who had worked, often for many years, in a once great, but now declining industry, and find them jobs in an area where unemployment was already high, and alternative opportunities were not terribly evident.

Swiftly they moved into action. Offices were acquired in the centre of Middlesbrough for company headquarters. At the yard itself, a job shop was opened. Everyday, cards advertising the latest vacancies were ferried out there and displayed. Men who had been shipyard workers were hastily retrained as job counsellors, whose task was to advise their workmates. Offices were provided for counselling sessions. Leaflets were issued. They carried a guarantee. It was not, unfortunately, that you would get a job to replace the one you had just lost. It was that 'we shall never give up trying to help you'. More specifically, it offered a number of services – financial advice on how to invest your redundancy money and on what unemployment or social security benefits you might be entitled to.

Then, if you despaired of finding work at home, and were resigned to becoming a part of Teesside's industrial diaspora, BSEL could offer information about your new home town, subsidised visits, help with accommodation, and even money towards removal expenses. It offered the chance to retrain, to upgrade existing skills, or acquire new ones, during which time the trainee would be paid 75 per cent of his or her normal pay. The company also offered a leg-up to those who wanted to join the 'enterprise culture' and start their own businesses. This, again, might be in the form of advice, training, accommodation, and even a little money.

As with a number of other nationalised industries in which drastic job reductions had taken place, the redundancy terms offered to shipyard workers were a good deal more generous than the minimum required by law. At Smith's Dock, permanent employees, which meant all but 150 of the workforce, were entitled to a package that comprised three or, in some cases, four different elements.

First, there was 13 weeks' pay in lieu of notice. Second, there was a closure bonus, amounting to 10 weeks' pay. This was conditional on the workforce's co-operation in the running down of the yard. Third, there was a lump sum redundancy payment. This arose from two sources. There was a statutory benefit based on age and length of service. This would amount to a maximum of 30 times weekly pay for a man of 61 or over, with more than 20 years' service. Naturally, those who were younger or had shorter lengths of service would get progressively less. British Shipbuilders' own scheme, however, enhanced this by providing a sum equivalent to two weeks' pay, multiplied by the individual's years of continuous service up to a maximum of 40 weeks' pay. There was a cash ceiling of £10,300 put on this payment, but this was too high to affect anyone below middle management level.

Under these schemes, the maximum total payment to a craftsman would be around £13,000. It was expected, though, that average payments would be about £6,000. This being an average, it naturally meant that, while some would receive more, others would get less.

For workers over 40, though, the fourth element of the package came into effect, reflecting, no doubt, the additional difficulties they could be expected to face in the labour market. This comprised a weekly support payment from British Shipbuilders, consisting of two weeks' pay for every year of service, up to a maximum of 20 years, divided by 104, and paid every week for two years. This was on the assumption that the worker remained unemployed. If he or she found work, then the support payment would be reduced; the aim being to bring the new wages up to the equivalent of 90 per cent of the money earned at Smith's Dock.

Such, then, was the safety net erected for the Smith's Dock workforce as it left the relatively secure conditions of the shipyard to face what few could deny was going to be a pretty bleak environment outside. After the announcement and the debates of May, the story soon faded from the headlines. It was no longer unusual to hear about major closures in British industries – not even in those in which we once led the world.

Ships number 1359 and 1360 remained on the slipways – the East Islands and the North Islands, last of a batch of four to be delivered to their Cuban owners – and Smith's Dock quietly worked itself out of a job. Every month from May onwards, workers were made redundant, at first voluntarily, until by October half had gone.

October 15th was the fateful day, when the last shipyard on the Tees was to launch its last ship. For the last time, Smith's Dock was again national headline news. Television cameras were there. Newspapers carried photographs featuring some individual worker, soon to be a dole queue statistic, with the great ship standing behind him.

Three thousand turned out to watch another melancholy episode in Britain's industrial (or was it post-industrial?) history. At 2.15 in the afternoon, on time to the second, the hydraulic trigger was released, and, without champagne or ceremony, the North Islands slipped, slowly at first, but with increasing power and majesty, into the Tees. For the last time at Smith's Dock, the waiting tugs got lines on board, tooted a salute, and pulled the new ship around to the berth where she would be fitted out and finished.

Managing director Roger Spence said: 'I believe the nation will live to regret what is happening because . . . when the upturn comes – as it is predicted by the 1990s – the industry will be too small to cope, and our ships will have to be built abroad.' Mr Spence had spent his whole working life – 40 years – at the yard, beginning as an apprentice draughtsman. He had said at the time the closure was announced, 'This is the worst day of my life.'

Mr Spence's loyalty to his employer, British Shipbuilders, probably prevented his speaking out more forcibly, but he added: 'We survived the Kaiser and Hitler and the economic crisis during the 1920s and 1930s, but we are not to survive 1986.' More ominous quotes, though, were available from the workforce: 'I am finished now. At my age

there is nothing here . . . God knows what next year holds . . . What I
fear is the boredom. I've seen active and agile men just fall apart.'
   Then Smith's Dock again passed into obscurity. What work there
was left continued to be done. On Fridays, some people would leave
the yard never to return, and the date for the final closure was set for
27 February 1987. Then, 10 days before Christmas, the story took an
extraordinary turn. It was, said the then Langbaurgh Council leader,
Arthur Seed, 'the best possible Christmas present' for Teesside.
   An unknown consortium, made up of an Englishman, two
Americans, and two Omanis, brought together by a Middlesbrough
ship surveyor, had agreed to buy the yard from British Shipbuilders
for £2.5 million. They were involved with the oil industry, and had
chosen Smith's Dock for their European base in an empire that was
planned to span the world, because of what one consortium member
described as the high level of technical excellence and traditional
skills to be found in the Teesside area. He added: 'We want to be good
citizens and provide a valuable asset within the community.'
Assurances were given that former Smith's Dock workers would have
priority when personnel were being selected for the new venture.
   Over the next few weeks, further details emerged of the ambitious
plans that the consortium had for the yard. The main activity would
be related to offshore oil, a field in which plenty of Teesside
companies already worked. In particular, it was planned to take
drilling rigs, and convert them into floating production platforms,
but this was to be only the beginning. Other ideas were soon leaking
out: they would build luxury yachts for the Arab market, they were to
make a concrete replica of a sailing ship to be hired out to film
makers, another venture would be the conversion of disused
containers to emergency homes for those stricken by earthquakes or
other natural disasters. They might even produce some of the cargo
ships that Smith's Dock had been building before its closure.
   As the plans grew more ambitious, so did the promised number of
jobs. This began with a fairly modest 200. Within days, though, it had
mounted to 360, with a promise of 600 before long. Then, on New
Year's Eve, the front page banner headline in the local paper, the
Evening Gazette, proclaimed '2,500 jobs at Smith's Dock'.
   The story had come from the New Year message of the Teesside
Conservative MP, Richard Holt. He said that, on the basis of figures
supplied to the Department of Industry by the consortium, there
would be 1,260 workers by the end of 1987, 1,812 by the end of 1988,
and 2,251 by the end of 1989. This would be a remarkable success
story, as the number of jobs being lost at Smith's Dock was less than

1,500. Mr Holt used it as evidence to back up his claim that 1987 would be the 'Year of the North'.

Cynics felt what was more significant was that it was almost certainly going to be election year. Some were no doubt puzzled to read that the offshore oil industry was going to create all these jobs at the yard, when it was being freely reported that, following the oil price collapse, 1987 was going to be an extremely tough year for the industry, with forecasts of thousands of jobs being *lost*. Little scepticism was expressed, though, except by a few Labour politicians. Perhaps it is hardly surprising that in an area that had had such an overdose of bad economic news, there was a marked reluctance to look this attractive gift horse in the mouth.

During the early weeks of January, everything went swimmingly with triumphant press conferences, news that 'final hurdles' were being overcome, and that, although the actual signing of the purchase contract had slipped back a little, it was on the point of being completed 'in the next few days', or, at worst, 'next week'.

It never was. On 22 January came another twist in the saga, as dramatic as the news that the yard was being rescued in the first place. This time, though, it was bad news. The consortium had split: the Omanis going one way, and the British-American faction the other. The root of the problem appeared to be a disagreement over how the shareholding was to be distributed, but there were also recriminations about a previous contract that the group had been involved with, and which had gone sour.

The row raged. The Omani side said the others had pulled out; they said they had not. The Omanis said they were providing the money, and so would go ahead with the purchase regardless. The British-American faction said they would take legal action to prevent the sale's going ahead without them, and, anyway, the yard could not survive without the contracts that they would bring to it. Throughout all this, the consortium managed to keep up a show of optimism, and the newspapers remained full of stories that the contract was about to be signed. A date was even set for the official opening.

In mid-February, the last ship sailed from Smith's Dock for Cuba. On 27 February, the yard closed. Still the saga continued. Worries arose about the effect this might be having on the former Smith's Dock workforce. There was a belief that some men might be pinning all their hopes on the re-opening of Smith's Dock, and not pursuing other possibilities. Indeed, in March, BSEL sent out 400 letters warning about this danger. The letter suggested that the consortium's plans might take a little time to come to fruition, and recipients were advised that it might be 'in their interests to look for other options in the interim'.

Eventually, British Shipbuilders' patience over the sale of the yard snapped, and, at the end of April, it went to the Tees and Hartlepool Port Authority. They had shown interest before the consortium appeared on the scene, but they were offering a lower price, and promising to create far fewer jobs. The Port Authority too were hoping to make a living from Smith's Dock from the offshore oil industry, by using it as a servicing base.

Even now, at the eleventh hour, a new dark horse came up on the rails. The ship surveyor who had put together the original consortium said that now an Anglo-American group, Offshore Capital Investment Inc, would outbid the Port Authority. They were going to build a £100 million import-export terminal, and production facilities to convert grain into food for animal and human consumption. They would also operate an offshore construction yard, and, for good measure, bring back shipbuilding. Legal action was even threatened to prevent the sale of the yard to the Port Authority, but it went ahead.

Much of the equipment in the yard was surplus to their requirements, and was auctioned off. There is a limited demand, though, for old industrial plant, so much of what had made Smith's Dock still recognisable as a shipyard was razed to the ground. It was a sad sight for those members of the old workforce who were aware that it was happening. Now they had to face up to the realities of the Teesside labour market, or rather the lack of one. The Port Authority took over the yard at the end of 1987, and might eventually produce useful employment, but, clearly, there was going to be no miracle.

The kind of experience that job seekers would face was illustrated by an incident in January 1987. A chemicals company just across the river from Middlesbrough advertised 12 vacancies. They got 5,000 applicants. The personnel manager said: 'We looked at the number of forms with shock, tinged with sadness . . . the terrible shame is that there are so many good people we won't be able to take on.'

CHAPTER 3

THE WORKFORCE

Teesside was always steeped in heavy industry and that's the declining part.
(Smith's Dock managing director)

One of the most striking things about the Smith's Dock workforce was its strong family tradition. Men often followed in grandfather's, father's, uncle's or brother's footsteps. Or wives would follow their husbands into the yard, or occasionally, it might be the other way around. When Teesside Polytechnic's interviewers began to question our representative sample of 200 Smith's Dock workers, it emerged that more than 20 per cent of our sample had another member of the family working at the yard when they started there. In happier days in the shipbuilding industry, when an apprenticeship at Smith's Dock was much sought after, it used to be said that only those who already had a relative working there were likely to be accepted.

For those who did have more than one member of the family working at the yard, of course, the blow of redundancy was even harder. The worst affected family in our sample was the one that suddenly learned it was going to lose three wage packets.

Until its closure, Smith's Dock had offered a steady job. Nearly half of the people in our sample had worked there for 10 years or more, and nearly 10 per cent had more than 30 years' service, the longest spell being 46 years. Now they were about to be pitched onto a labour market where steady jobs were becoming ever scarcer, as casual work increased, so that a high proportion of the few jobs that were available, especially in manufacturing, were on short-term contracts.

Table 1 *Length of service at Smith's Dock (in years)*

	%
Up to 5	21
5 – 9	34
10 – 20	29
21 – 30	7
31 – 40	7
More than 40	2

The workforce was not starry-eyed about Smith's Dock. Many of the sample complained that the work was badly-paid, dirty or even dangerous. More than a quarter spoke of 'poor working conditions', and there were also common complaints about the harsh weather conditions and the attitude of management. However, 20 per cent of those we questioned said they could think of nothing bad about working at Smith's Dock.

Table 2 *The bad things about working at Smith's Dock*

	%
Poor working conditions	28
Dislike attitude of management	19
Harsh weather conditions	19
Others	14
No bad things	21

Smith's Dock did not have a reputation for paying high wages. Of the workers we interviewed, more than a third were earning £100 a week or less, and less than 20 per cent were getting more than £140 a week, with only a handful on more than £180.

Table 3 *Average pay from Smith's Dock (in pounds per week)*

	%
Up to 70	5
71 – 100	29
101 – 140	47
141 – 180	15
More than 180	4

In spite of the harshness of working conditions, the unexciting financial rewards, and the ups and ever more common downs in shipbuilding, however, Smith's Dock offered the prospect of a guaranteed pay packet at the end of the week. Perhaps that is why 16 per cent of our interviewees told us that they had left the yard at some point in their working life, only to return later. Three individuals said they had left on four occasions, but returned each time, and one claimed to have had no less than eight spells at the yard! Even more striking was that, after being made redundant, 70 per cent said that if Smith's Dock re-opened, they would like to return.

Unemployment was not a new experience for many of the people in the sample. Not surprisingly, in view of Teesside's recent economic history, 43 per cent had been unemployed before, some several times. Sixteen people had already been long-term unemployed – out of work for a year or more – while four people had previously been unemployed for more than four years. In addition, a number had also had first-hand experience of a shipyard closure: one in ten had been transferred from the nearby Haverton Hill shipyard, when it was closed in the late seventies.

The workforce was very short of educational qualifications. Of our sample, 55 per cent had left school without any. Only one person had a degree, only two had 'A' levels, and only ten had any 'O' levels. This clearly could not be helpful in trying to find work.

In terms of industrial skills, though, the workforce appeared to be reasonably well qualified. Sixty-five per cent had done an apprentice-ship, and another 6 per cent had received other specific job training. The problem was whether the skill they had acquired was likely to be in demand outside the yard. Some trades were specific to ship-building, like those of the shipwright or the caulker/burner. They formed more than 10 per cent of our sample.

In another category came trades like welding and plating: more readily transferable, but still specific to traditional manufacturing industry. They made up around a quarter of the sample. Another sector of the manual workforce comprised people like plumbers, joiners, or electricians, who should have skills that would be in demand outside manufacturing. They accounted for about 6 per cent.

Just less than a fifth of the workforce were white collar workers. There were some from the large drawing office, which had quite advanced computer-aided equipment, as well as clerks and the various grades of management. The expectation was that they would, on the whole, fare better in finding new jobs.

As in any shipyard, most of the workers at Smith's Dock were men. In fact, there were only about 60 women employed there, fewer than 5 per cent of the total workforce. They were to be found cleaning, working in the canteen or being secretaries or wages clerks.

Table 4 *Main occupations of sample*

	%
Welders	14
Platers	10
Fitters	8
Labourers	8
Foremen/supervisors	7
Shipwrights	6
Caulker/burners	5
Crane/transport drivers	5
Secretaries/clerical	5
Management	5
Joiners	4
Canteen staff	4

In terms of age range, the workers were fairly evenly distributed. More than a third were under 30, but, at the other end of the age range, more than a fifth were over 50.

Table 5 *Ages of sample members*

	%
Under 30	36
30 – 39	25
40 – 49	18
50 – 59	15
60 +	6

Most members of our sample were married or lived with a partner – 73 per cent. Seventeen per cent were single, and 10 per cent divorced or separated. The vast majority of the workforce – 71 per cent – were owner-occupiers. Seventeen per cent rented council houses, 1 per cent rented from a private landlord, and the rest lived with parents or relatives.

At the time when we were compiling this information, during our first round of interviews in December 1986 and January 1987, the phased closure was in progress. Some had already left, some were about to leave, and others knew they would have to stay on until or almost until the bitter end, as Smith's Dock slowly died around them.

Reactions to the closure were predictably negative, with 80 per cent of the sample subscribing to feelings ranging from sadness to disgust. It was perhaps a mark of how persistent the rumours of closure had been over the years that only 20 per cent said they were shocked or surprised. Among the more picturesque comments were, 'I felt I'd been hit with a sledge hammer', 'It was cold-blooded the way in which the closure was announced. It was like a knife going into the heart of the area.' 'At a quarter to twelve I was reassuring a lad that we wouldn't close this time, at twelve we were shutting.'

Some saw it as a further example of the North-South divide, then becoming a topic of national political controversy: 'It's just another nail in the coffin. We're not cared about around here. There's another 1,500 jobs gone and no one cares.'

On the other hand, 6 per cent said they had mixed feelings about the closure, 5 per cent said they were not bothered, and a further 5 per cent even said they were excited or glad. Individual comments give a clue to the feelings behind these sentiments. 'It was an antiquated yard. In wet conditions, with electrical equipment all over, it was a death trap.' 'In a way, it's good to have to look for a different job. We were living in the past too much. Poor working conditions, old-fashioned ideas, poor management – they caused the yard to close.' Or, more simply, 'I'm looking forward to spending the redundancy money.'

Many complained that the closure was 'political'. They seemed to mean that the yard was not shut primarily for economic or organisational reasons, but because it was believed that Teessiders would not kick up too much of a fuss. A large proportion of the workforce believed, rightly or wrongly, that Smith's Dock was a good deal more efficient than some other yards that had been allowed to remain open.

On the subject of politics, there was also a rather cynical, but widely-held view that, with a general election approaching, voters in safe Labour seats should not look for any government hand-outs, and that these would be reserved for marginals in an effort to help the Conservatives get re-elected. It is true that most of the local seats were Labour-held, but in Langbaurgh, the Conservative Richard Holt was having to defend a majority of only 6,000.

Whatever the foundation for this suspicion, we did ask our sample how they voted in the general election of 1983, and then that of 1987. On each occasion only 12 per cent voted Conservative, but the closure did not help Labour's cause, in spite of its strong criticism of the decision. The number of Labour voters dropped from 60 per cent in 1983 to only 53 per cent four years later, with the Alliance picking up the difference.

During this first round of interviews, we also decided to get a snapshot of how people viewed their now uncertain futures. What was the balance between hope and apprehension? In fact, people's assessment of the local labour market was such that only 44 per cent expected to be working in six months' time.

Table 6 *How long interviewees believed it would take to find a suitable job (in months)*

	%
Up to 2	13
Up to 6	31
Up to 12	28
More than 12	28

More than a third of those interviewed said they were 'unhappy' or 'very concerned' about the future, though only 7 per cent fewer, 29 per cent, said they were happy or reasonably happy about it. It is worth noting that this was the time when the story that the yard was about to be rescued by an Arab-American consortium was making headline news in the local papers.

None the less, people were already working out their strategies for surviving what might turn out to be an austere financial climate. 'In the long-term, if no job is forthcoming, we shall cut back on non-essentials like the car and the telephone.' 'I know mum is buying me clothes for Christmas to help keep me going.' Others made an immediate connection between shortage of money and the possibility of increased tensions in the family.

'There's a tendency to quarrel over financial matters. It causes tensions when we are under one another's feet.' 'It's made me moody, caused arguments. I couldn't make plans for holidays, or buying a new car. Can't start a family.' 'At the moment, mum and dad are feeding me and clothing me. For a bloke my age, this is not a good feeling. I should be starting to think about supporting my own family.'

There was a widespread belief among those interviewed that what they could look forward to was a future of unemployment, where money would be short, and life would be blighted by boredom and quarrels with loved ones. 'I'll die of boredom if I don't get another job.' 'It could be a problem if I end up on the dole and we are under one another's feet, we might end up fighting.' 'The wife and I argue a lot more.' 'My family take a lot of stick. I take it out on them.' 'I'm on a short fuse, bad-tempered.'

Another problem for men was the loss of the self-esteem that went with the job. 'I feel depressed because I'm not the breadwinner.' This feeling might be particularly stong if the wife or partner had a job. 'She'll be the breadwinner. It could cause conflict.'

Some felt that the financial problems would be staved off, at least for a time, by the redundancy payments. For those who had been lucky enough to find a new job, the redundancy payments were quite

a bonus. 'We are in a good way financially. I now have capital in the
bank. Because I'm working I don't need to touch that. As a family we
feel a lot more secure.'

Those who found that the redundancy money had relieved their
financial problems felt that family life had improved, just as those
who were short of money felt it had been adversely affected. 'It has
relieved the financial stress so, therefore, we are more relaxed . . . As
far as our family life is concerned, it is very much better, and my wife
and I have a lot more time together.' For those who did not face
financial problems, the idea of more free time promised an enrich-
ment of life. 'I will find a lot more time on my hands to do the things I
have always wanted to do and hopefully can afford to do. I will have
more time to take my grandchildren to the park.'

For some who left the yard early, though, with a small redundancy
pay-out, the money had run out even before Smith's Dock finally
closed. 'The redundancy money was good while it lasted. We bought
some things – a washer and a fridge/freezer. We can't afford to run
the car. Something went wrong and I can't afford to put it right.' For
these people, finding a job soon took on a desperate urgency.

CHAPTER 4

LOOKING FOR WORK

> *I didn't realise it would be so*
> *difficult to get a job.*
>
> (Barry Reed)

So we have a workforce that was stable, long-serving, not particularly youthful, reasonably well-trained, but in skills that were acquired for a dying industry. How would it make out as it was dumped, more than 1,400 strong, on a labour market where manufacturing had been in headlong retreat for years, and where the unemployment rate was well over 20 per cent?

As we have seen, the rundown of Smith's Dock was phased over a number of months, and the first round of interviewing was completed before the yard was closed. The second round started around the time of the final closure at the end of February 1987, after which only a handful of people were left at the yard to do maintenance and book-keeping. At that time, 65 per cent of those questioned were unemployed, and only 21 per cent were in work (the remainder being in training or education, or sick or retired).

As table 7 shows, the number unemployed steadily declined as time went on, and the number in work correspondingly increased. By Christmas 1987, the numbers were almost equal, and by the summer of 1988, the situation of February 1987 had been virtually reversed, with 65 per cent now employed, against 23 per cent who were unemployed. None the less, this meant that 18 months after the yard closed, more than a fifth of those who lost their jobs had still not been absorbed by the Cleveland labour market. This is in spite of a fall in the unemployment rate in the county from nearly 22 per cent at the time of the closure to just over 16 per cent by the middle of 1988.

Table 7 *Employment status*

	Round 2 (%)	Round 3 (%)	Round 4 (%)	Round 6 (%)	Round 7 (%)	Round 8 (%)
Employed	21	24	27	39	56	65
Unemployed	65	60	58	40	30	23
In training/education	4	10	5	12	4	1
Sick/retired	10	6	10	9	10	11

To some degree, it is possible to use the fortunes of our sample as a barometer for the overall state of the Teesside, or even the national, economy, but taking the raw figures for the number in work versus the number out of work may not give a completely reliable picture. First, it is important to remember that, in many ways, the former shipyard workers were a favoured group compared with the rest of the unemployed on Teesside. (This may be a sobering thought when it is seen how much unhappiness the closure caused.) As we have seen, they had the benefit, in BSEL, of a job-finding apparatus set up specifically for them. They had their criticisms of it, but it was more than the rest of the unemployed on Teesside got.

Second, the quality of many of the jobs they found was dubious. The hours might be long, the conditions might be poor, the pay might be low, and the security might be nil. (We will be examining the kind of jobs that people got in chapter 11.)

In view of the obvious difficulties of the labour market on Teesside, one of the things we wanted to discover was where and how enthusiastically people looked for jobs. One measure of this would be how often unemployed people went to the job centre. The number of those saying they had visited the job centre was rather lower at the time of the final closure than it was just over a year later. This may have been to do with the high hopes at that time that the Arab-American consortium was about to re-open the yard, or with the amount of information about new jobs that could be found at the yard itself, making it less necessary to go to a job centre. Of the 85 per cent who said they had been going to the job centre in the spring of 1988, just under half said they went once a week or more.

Table 8 *Percentage of unemployed who had visited the job centre since the last interview*

Round 2	63
Round 7	85

It is something of a testimony to people's determination to find work that so many did go to the job centre regularly, even though a large, and growing, majority felt that it was not useful. The most common cause for complaint was that there were either 'no jobs' or 'no suitable jobs' advertised, rather than any shortcomings in the organisation.

Table 9 *Value of the job centre*

	Useful (%)	Not useful (%)
Round 2	33	67
Round 7	23	77

The Polytechnic identified 30 interviewees as having staff status at Smith's Dock. Eight of them said they had registered with Professional and Executive Recruitment. One said they had found PER useful, and five said that they had not.

Apart from examining how often they went to the job centre, we also asked the unemployed regular questions about how many jobs they had applied for. There was consistently a group of 40 per cent or more who said they had not applied for any since they were last interviewed. When asked why they had not applied for jobs, the most common answer was that there were few, if any, available. The proportion who had not been applying for jobs declined as time went on. This might be a reflection of a picking-up in the labour market that we have noted above, or it might reflect a growing desperation as redundancy money ran out. Equally, the unemployed were not an unchanging group – there was a constant movement in and out of work in an increasingly casualised labour market (see chapter 11). The number who had been unemployed ever since the yard closed was down to around 15 per cent by the spring of 1988, so it would be rash to conclude that the failure to apply for jobs resulted from workshyness.

In many ways what is more striking is the consistent and growing proportion of people who applied for more than 10, 20 or even 50 jobs. For those who have never been unemployed, it is hard to imagine the degree of determination and emotional stamina that is required to keep on applying for jobs in the face of constant disappointment and rejection, not to mention the difficulty of finding any jobs for which to apply. We put this point to our sample: did they agree with the statement 'Given the current employment situation in this area, people can get used to being unemployed and stop looking for work'? Eight-one per cent agreed (see chapter 5, table 18).

Table 10 *Jobs applied for since the previous interview*

	Round 2 (%)	Round 5 (%)	Round 6 (%)	Round 8 (%)
None	54	56	47	43
1–2	20	20	22	18
3–5	18	11	13	20
6–10	3	6	8	5
11–20	4	3	6	10
21–50	1	3	3	2
51 +	0	1	1	2

One individual told us he had applied for 90 jobs since the last interview. These kind of scores can easily be run up by people who are in a job club, a Government-backed scheme whereby unemployed people go to a club which provides them with some resources for their job search. These include basic training in how to look, and access to stationery, a typewriter, trade directories and a telephone. Each member of the club is then supposed to follow up 10 job leads a day. What this tends to mean in practice is sending off large numbers of unsolicited curricula vitae to companies who might or, more likely, might not be looking for staff. By the end of 1987, 23 per cent of the unemployed, 17 people, were or had been members of a job club Three said they had found jobs as a result.

At first, the main source of information about jobs for the unemployed was family or friends, but, as time went on, advertisements and the job centre tended to take over. It is dangerous to be too specific about this pattern, as many interviewees were unclear about where the information about particular jobs had come from. Nevertheless, there does appear to be a contrast between the unemployed and those who found work (see chapter 11, table 36). For the latter, friends and family were clearly the most common source for the job in which they were working. In other words, those most likely to find work were, perhaps, those with the most influential, or best-informed, friends and family. This would bear out a commonly-voiced sentiment on Teesside. When it comes to getting a job, 'It's not what you know, it's who you know.'

The unemployed are sometimes accused of being too choosy in their search for work. So we asked our interviewees what kind of job they were looking for? Half of those out of work said they were looking for any job that was available. At one point, we asked our interviewees whether they agreed with a list of statements read to them. One was 'Any job is better than being on the dole'; 42 per cent said they agreed with this statement.

Table 11 *Percentage of unemployed who have applied for jobs using information from these sources since the last interview*

	Round 2 (%)	Round 5 (%)	Round 6 (%)	Round 8 (%)
Family/friend	35	16	35	14
Advertisement	33	13	22	50
Job centre	12	20	19	32
Shipyard/BSEL	8	7	3	0
Applied 'on spec'	6	4	0	9

Note: interviewees might choose more than one category.

It is also suggested that people find themselves out of work because their expectations of what a job should pay are too high, that they 'price themselves out of a job', and that in order to get work, they should lower these expectations and 'price themselves into a job'. We tried to establish, therefore, just what kind of pay rates the unemployed were expecting. We found that their demands were extremely modest. More than half said they expected net pay of £100 a week or less, and only two people (4 per cent) wanted more than £150 a week. Everyone would have been prepared to take a job at £180 a week.

Table 12 *Minimum acceptable weekly pay after tax*

£	%
approx 50	8
51–90	18
100	27
110	2
120	16
130	12
140	4
150	10
160	2
180	2

So it is interesting to note that 69 people, 39 per cent of the sample, said that they had turned down jobs since leaving Smith's Dock. A wide variety of reasons was given, but the most common was that the pay was too low. In view of the very modest financial expectations of those looking for work, it does make one wonder exactly what pay rates were on offer in these jobs.

As time went on, the views of the unemployed on how quickly they would get another job began to change. At the time of the closure, more than a third said that they thought it was likely they would be working in six months' time. By May 1987, however, when it was beginning to be clear that the Arab-American consortium's plans to buy the yard had fallen through, the proportion went down to just over a quarter.

As optimism declined, pessimism took over. Shortly after the final closure, 7 per cent of the unemployed said they thought it would take them a year or more to find a job. Two months later, this had more than doubled. As we moved into 1988, and unemployment continued to fall, there seemed to be a re-birth of optimism. It is worth noting, though, that in the summer of 1988, the proportion of the unemployed who thought they would never get another job was at its highest level, at more than one in seven, perhaps reflecting the discouragement born of constant rejection, and a persistent lack of suitable vacancies. In addition to those who thought they would never get a job, there was a fairly constant proportion of around 40 per cent of the unemployed who said they did not know how long it would take them to find one. This too may be a comment on the scarcity of jobs available.

Table 13 *How long the unemployed thought it would take to find a job*

	Round 2 (%)	Round 3 (%)	Round 6 (%)	Round 7 (%)
Up to 2 months	8	8	19	24
Up to 6 months	26	18	22	6
Up to 12 months	9	9	7	4
More than 12 months	7	16	3	8
Don't know	45	36	42	45
Don't think I'll ever get one	5	12	7	14

In the summer of 1988 we conducted separate interviews with the spouses and partners of our sample members. We asked them similar questions about how long the search for a job might take. Thirty-six per cent said they did not know, and 15 per cent said they did not think their partner would ever get another job.

In addition to job clubs, the Government initiated a number of other schemes to help the unemployed back to work. These included the Enterprise Allowance scheme in which people who sign off the dole to start their own business can get £40 a week for their first year, and, notably, the Community Programme. This was generally available to those who had been out of work for a year, and provided what was usually part-time, low-paid work for a limited period of time.

There was clearly a high degree of cynicism about these schemes, with 60 per cent of the sample saying they viewed them unfavourably. (One frequent complaint about the job centres was that the only jobs advertised were Community Programme.) In the spring of 1988, we asked those still unemployed whether they thought they would like to apply for a place on the new Employment Training scheme (ET) then about to be launched. Seventy-three per cent said they would not be interested. (At the time of writing, the Government are still stressing that this will be a voluntary scheme, while critics are arguing that those who decline places will find their benefits stopped or reduced, and that ET will effectively become compulsory.)

Another Government initiative introduced nationally in 1987 was Re-start, a scheme whereby the long-term unemployed were helped to get back into work. That at least is how it was described in the publicity; critics claimed it was designed to frighten and harass the unemployed into stopping claiming benefits, which saved money, and had the added advantage of removing them from the jobless figures.

By the autumn of 1987, we found that 41 per cent of the unemployed had been called to a Re-start interview. Of those, roughly equal numbers said they found it 'useful' and 'not useful'. By the end of the year, half of all the unemployed had been called in, but no one reported getting a job as a result.

Neither had the various government bodies charged with helping to revive the Teesside economy made very much of an impact. In the autumn of 1987, we asked our interviewees for their views on the Middlesbrough Task Force and the newly-created Teesside Development Corporation. Three quarters said they had not heard of them.

As we have seen, by the summer of 1988, there had been a clear reduction in the number of people reported to be out of work in Cleveland. None the less, many of the sample – 39 per cent – said they could see no overall improvement, as against 44 per cent who said they could. Twelve per cent said that efforts were being made to give the 'impression' of an improvement, but they were not sure what exactly was supposed to be improving.

As time went on, more and more of the unemployed began to feel that their age was proving a barrier to their getting a job. In the spring of 1987, only 12 per cent said they did, but by the winter of 1987, half of the unemployed were taking this view. The majority who said age was a problem were over 40, but nearly a quarter were only in their thirties. A quarter of the unemployed complained that job advertisements often contained age restrictions, usually affecting those over

35. At the end of 1987, we analysed the ages of those who were still
unemployed to see whether age really was a problem in getting a job.
The answer seemed to bear out these fears. Of those aged over 45,
three quarters were out of work.

Case study

Barry Reed is a 48-year-old shipwright. He had two spells of work at
Smith's Dock. The first lasted 26 years. Then he took redundancy in
1979 to nurse his sick wife. After she died, he had a spell out of work.
Then he got a labouring job at British Steel, cleaning the coke ovens,
though that lasted for only a short time. Eventually, he was given the
chance to return to the shipyard as a temporary worker. He worked at
the yard for 11 months, until he lost his job in October 1986.

As a temporary worker, Barry was not entitled to a redundancy
payment this time. All he received was 13 weeks' pay in lieu of notice.
Nor were temporary workers – of whom there were about 150 at
Smith's Dock – eligible for assistance from BSEL in finding work.

Barry has two sons, and lives in a bungalow, on which he has a
small mortgage, on a pleasant new housing estate beneath the Eston
Hills. As with so many of those I interviewed, the first thing that hit
Barry about being unemployed was the boredom.

> It's a job finding things to fill your time. They're very long days,
> and you have to do a hobby – inexpensive hobbies, like crosswords
> or jigsaws – to fill your time in. I do the housework and that, with
> being by myself, and that does take a bit of your time, doing a little
> bit of shopping, and then I fall back to the jigsaws, crosswords,
> things like that. Especially winter time; winter comes, there's snow
> on the ground, you can't get out. I think that's when your days
> seem very long. Summer, it's nice – you can go out.
>
> When you were at Smith's Dock, you were there half past seven
> till four. The day passed pretty quick. When you came home, by
> the time you'd pottered about in the garden, done little jobs like
> that, then your day was full. And if you wanted a couple of pints
> afterwards, that was ideal.

Again, in common with so many others, Barry found that the
shortage of money made it even more difficult to fill up the days.

> First of all, I'd had my redundancy seven years ago, so I have no

complaints about that. But it does cause problems now, because on unemployment benefit, I'm getting £32 a week, and that does really make it hard to live on – £32 a week – and yet people, you know, some of these ministers say 'Well, it's a living wage.' It's not a living wage. Nobody can live on £32 a week. I certainly can't.
  If you have money you can always get out and enjoy yourself, go places. But with unemployment benefit, you certainly can't. You have to watch your pennies, and the bills – that's the main thing. You try to get your gas, electricity, stuff like that paid. It's difficult at times.

Barry understood that the skills he had to offer, as a shipwright, were unlikely to be in demand in an area where shipbuilding had been virtually wiped out. 'Out of the shipyards, you can't follow it on – well, it's very difficult I should say. So, it would have to be a labouring job – driving, storeman, something like that.'
  In the event, looking for a job proved difficult to impossible.

I didn't realise it would be so difficult to get a job, but now I know the market. I've wrote after jobs. Sometimes you get replies. Most of the time you don't. You can understand the employer, because there must be thousands of people applying for jobs. But it's a little bit demoralising at times. I think it'd cheer you up if you did get a reply back, although you didn't get the job. I go in the job centre regularly – there's not much else you can do, really.

Barry felt that the crucial difficulty that he faced was his age.

I think once you reach an age over 44 or 45, I think you then have difficulty finding work. You feel as though you're thrown on the scrapheap, and they go for the younger people. You can't blame the employer. He wants a younger, fitter man, so he'll take a young person. But it's a bit tragic. A 48-year-old. I've got 17 years before a pension, and it's a long time to be unemployed, 17 years. It's a crying shame. I think I have a lot to offer.

Barry is not prone to drama and exaggeration. The possibility that he might never get another job is, to him, quite real:

I can't see it getting any better, unless a large employer comes in, and there's nothing on the horizon for that. Because unemployment in this area's so large, it's tremendous. It'll take a thousand jobs just to make an inroad into the unemployment in this area.

His despondency over his own predicament, however, does not
blind Barry to the problem of others. In particular, he feels that the
plight of those considered too old in their forties is less serious than
that of young people who cannot find work. 'I think at 40, you
certainly have the experience, but when you look back at it, I feel
sorry for the youngsters who've never had a job.'

Among them is Barry's younger son, Derek. His elder son, also
named Barry, has gone to work down south. His younger son
followed him in an effort to find a job.

> The oldest lad, he went to London three years ago. He left
> university, and he got fixed up in London with a job which was no
> difficulty, because he had the qualifications.
>
> The youngest lad, he's 21 now, and all the work he's ever had is
> Community Programme jobs. He's just gone down to London.
> He's stopping with Barry at the moment, to see if he can get a job
> himself. But at the moment, he's had no luck. He's had no
> experience, really. I think that's the drawback for the lad.

The departure of his two sons brought Barry into contact with
another of the problems of unemployment – loneliness.

> I knew one would have to go, because he went to university, but
> then, the youngest lad, I was a bit sorry and a bit downhearted to
> see him go. I mean you've had them round the house for 21 years,
> you're bound to miss them, and with being by myself, it's a bit quiet
> around the house now.
>
> It's a shame you can't get jobs in this area, but he's only one of
> many. I mean there's lads in this area – 22, 23 years old, never had
> work at all. Only Community Programme jobs, but real jobs,
> never. It's a damn shame.

What he regards as the absence of opportunities for young people
on Teesside fills Barry with foreboding about the area's future. 'To
me, there's very little future for the area. I mean when you take young
people away from the area, I think that's what an area needs, young
people.'

Barry has absolutely no doubt that there is a North-South divide.

> I think for the people in the north of England, it is tragic, because
> there is a divide. I mean there's no bitterness against the southern
> people. We're all British people, we are a British nation, but they
> could put employment up north. We need it desperately up here.

The work is down in the south of England. When you have people emigrating down to the South, I think that is so tragic. I think firms could be persuaded to move north. I wish the politicians would listen to the people in the north of England, when we tell them there is a divide here. I wish the politicians would realise it, and not skate round it. The politicians that live in this area know what it's like, but it doesn't seem to do any good down the South. People in power just don't listen to them.

In spite of Barry's bleak view of Teesside's future, he does not see himself ever leaving the area. That is partly because of the genuine affection in which he holds it:

I really like the area. You've got the hills behind, the seaside five miles away, so you can't go wrong. I walk the dog in the hills. It gives me a bit of exercise and it gives the dog a little bit of exercise as well, and it passes a lot of time away. It's lovely in the summer when they're all green. I mean I might be biased because I've lived here all my life, but it's really a nice area.

There are economic reasons too, though:

I just couldn't afford to move. To buy any property in the south of England, I just wouldn't have the money. How can people afford to go and live in the south of England? Even if they sell a house, or even if they've paid for their house, I mean house prices are so different from north to south. You most probably have to borrow £20,000 or £30,000 again, and I don't think people of 40 or 50 would want to start that again. I think one mortgage is enough.

The cruellest thing for Barry now is the disappointment of hopes nurtured during the 30 years of his working life.

My idea of it was as soon as the lads are working and old enough to look after themselves, then you could start enjoying life, because you'd done your part. You'd brought them up properly, and then you can start having your holidays.
Because I don't think the working man asks for a lot. A car or something like that, and a holiday every year. I don't think that's a lot to ask for when you've worked all your life. I mean they're not really luxuries, are they, compared to other people? They're just the simple things. But unemployment turns all that around. We won't get anything like that.

Now Barry has re-married. His younger son, Derek, came back from London. 'He said there were jobs, but the money wasn't good enough to pay for somewhere to live.' Derek, though, did at least get a job on the Community Programme. Barry himself is now on sickness benefit as the result of an old back injury sustained at Smith's Dock in 1978. He had to have a disc removed, but that did not solve the problem. 'I don't think shovelling coke at British Steel or going back to Smith's Dock helped. If I walk too much it plays me up, or if I sit down too much.'

Tragically for Barry, he was offered the chance to return to Smith's Dock early in 1988 when ship repairing returned to the yard but had to turn down the job on doctor's orders. 'The doctor told me that if I wasn't careful I might end up in a wheelchair.'

CHAPTER 5

ON THE DOLE

I used to think people on the
dole didn't want to work.

(Les Hill)

What was the best thing about working at Smith's Dock? When we put that question to our interviewees, the answer was not the money or the security, but the companionship – an answer given by 41 per cent. Perhaps this helps to explain why, in the early months of unemployment, the psychological effects seemed more pronounced than the financial effects. At this time, of course, many people were cushioned by redundancy payments.

Table 14 *The 'good' things about working at Smith's Dock*

	%
Companionship/good workmates	43
Good atmosphere/job satisfaction	20
Regular wage	19
Pride in the work	11
Work was close to home	3
Others	3
No good things	2

A similar point was illustrated in the summer of 1987, six months after the yard had closed, when we asked unemployed interviewees what pressures they felt on them to find a job. The main one quoted was 'personal pride', which emerged as more important than 'financial pressures'. A year later, though, nearly two-thirds chose 'money' as the reason for wanting a job, far outnumbering all other reasons, like 'boredom', 'self-esteem', or 'security'. When, at the same interview, the unemployed were asked what was the worst thing about not having a job, lack of money was again the thing most commonly quoted, though this time by less than half, with nearly a third choosing boredom or lack of routine.

Table 15 *Pressures to get a job (summer 1987)*

	%
Personal pride	44
Financial pressures	39
Fear of being unable to adapt to work	2
Other	14

Table 16 *Main reason for wanting a job (summer 1988)*

	%
Money	63
Security	19
Self-respect	10
Lack of routine/boredom	8

Table 17 *The worst thing about not having a job (summer 1988)*

	%
Lack of money	43
Lack of routine/boredom	32
Insecurity	13
Depression/feeling degraded	6
Other	6

Sadly, as you might expect, the comradeship between workmates soon withered when daily contact at the workplace came to an end, so that by the spring of 1987, 22 per cent of the sample complained that they had lost contact with friends they had had at Smith's Dock. By the summer of 1988, this figure had risen to 28 per cent, and 58 per cent of the unemployed also said that they had not made new friends since leaving the yard.

There are a number of reasons why former Smith's Dock workers who had not found work might find it difficult to maintain friendships with workmates who now had new jobs. One is that unemployed people tend to be less mobile, and that, if they do go out, they face the embarrassment of not, for instance, being able to afford to buy a round of drinks when it is their turn. Another is that work forms such a large part of our lives, that often employed and unemployed find that they have nothing in common. So, by the summer of 1987, 12 per cent of the unemployed people in the sample

To try to reach an assessment of people's overall state of mind, we asked them to complete the General Health Questionnaire four times during the interviewing. The first occasion was around the time of the final closure of the yard, and the last in the summer of 1988. This involved putting a dozen questions like 'Do you feel constantly under strain?' 'Do you feel you have not been able to face up to your problems?' The more 'noes' you score, the better your mental state; the more 'yeses' the worse. The Polytechnic then analysed the answers.

The result was that on every single indicator the results from the employed showed a decreasing number of 'yeses' as time went on. Among the unemployed, on the other hand, every indicator except two showed an increasing number of 'yeses'. 'Have you been feeling unhappy and depressed?' and 'Have you been losing confidence in yourself?' showed particularly large increases, with about 40 per cent of the unemployed saying they had these feelings. A consistently large proportion also said they did not feel they were playing a useful part in things, though fewer generally said they did not think of themselves as useful people.

In the autumn of 1987, 30 per cent of those out of work, 32 individuals, said they felt that their health or that of their family had been affected. While eight quoted positive changes, like the absence of stress, or not working in a polluted environment, the rest quoted negative changes, most commonly depression.

We also tried to find out how spouses or partners were affected by our interviewees' being unemployed. More than half said it was difficult to cope, and more than a quarter said they felt their own health had been affected. Nineteen of those who were not working full-time were asked how their husband would feel if they had a part-time job. Eleven said either that he would object, or that it would make him feel inadequate. As we saw in chapter 3, a number of men were worried about the effect it might have on them if their wife or partner became the family breadwinner. There are still a significant minority on Teesside who believe that a woman's place is in the home. For example, 21 per cent of the sample said that a woman should only go out to work if it was absolutely necessary to support the family, and 10 per cent disagreed with the statement that there was no reason why a woman should not be the breadwinner.

Another significant non-financial effect of unemployment was that men who were used to being out of the house for a large part of their waking hours now found themselves at home 24 hours a day. Equally, a wife used to having the house to herself might now find the constant

Table 19 *The effect of unemployment on people's state of mind*

What interviewees said they had experienced	Employed (%)				Unemployed (%)			
	Round 2	Round 4	Round 6	Round 8	Round 2	Round 4	Round 6	Round 8
Reduced concentration on tasks	15	5	4	4	18	14	15	18
Loss of much sleep due to worry	15	8	10	10	12	12	17	19
Not playing a useful part in things	15	11	11	4	32	37	41	34
Inability to make decisions about things	7	3	4	0	6	10	13	16
Feeling constantly under strain	26	16	23	22	18	22	30	32
Inability to overcome difficulties	11	4	4	3	6	15	13	16
Inability to enjoy day-to-day activities	22	23	27	11	26	22	37	30
Inability to face up to problems	7	0	3	1	7	7	10	8
Feeling unhappy and depressed	19	14	16	10	20	27	37	39
Loss of confidence in one's self	15	10	9	1	13	17	23	40
Not thinking of oneself as a useful person	22	4	3	2	15	8	10	6
Not feeling happy, all things considered	22	10	14	4	24	20	26	19

presence of a husband or partner something of an intrusion on her territory. As one unemployed white collar worker put it,

She's said to me I'm invading her territory. I think she's right. I used to go to work at half past eight in the morning till half past four at night. She never used to see me five days a week. Now all that's changed. I'm in seven days a week, from eight o'clock in the morning till eleven o'clock at night, when I go to bed. Obviously I'm going to invade her territory. We argue a lot more than we used to. I suppose I get under her feet.

This complaint that spouses and partners 'got under each other's feet' cropped up time and time again in our interviews. The situation was no doubt made worse because opportunities for going for a night out, say, were reduced, either because money was already short, or because it was feared it soon would be. So in the months just after the yard closed, unemployed interviewees reported a sharp decline in 'going out', but an even sharper growth in the home-based activity of watching television.

Table 20 *Change in activities for the unemployed*

	Doing less		Doing more	
	Going out	Watching TV	Going out	Watching TV
	(%)	(%)	(%)	(%)
Round 2	35	8	10	57
Round 3	35	11	8	48

Here then was a cocktail that could be lethal to relationships – loneliness, boredom, claustrophobia, with an undercurrent of worries about money and uncertainty about the future. Then throw in loss of self-esteem and purpose in life, frustration on the part of the unemployed man because he could not find a job, and on the part of his partner or spouse because, from time to time, she felt he was not trying hard enough, or that he was not sufficiently resourceful. No wonder that 19 per cent of the sample volunteered the information that since the closure, they had had more family rows. When interviewees were asked for their reaction to the statement 'unemployment can break up family relationships', there was almost unanimous agreement (see table 18 above). It is also worth noting that one in twenty of the unemployed had at least one other unemployed person living in the household, which might also play a part in increasing tension.

Four members of our sample had their marriage break up during the 18 months after Smith's Dock closed. Another five, incidentally, found their plans to get married being interfered with by their being made redundant.

Some, though, saw having more time with the family as a bonus, and others enjoyed the opportunity to pursue interests outside work. So 24 per cent told us they enjoyed more freedom or time to relax and pursue their hobbies. A similar proportion reported having developed closer ties with their children. Only one person said their relationship with their children had been strained, while two others said their children were confused about why their father was not working.

Generally, though, there was considerable apprehension about the future among the unemployed. In the autumn of 1987, more than 80 per cent of the unemployed felt there was little or no future for themselves on Teesside, and a similar proportion felt there was little or no future for their children. The remainder, though, said they saw a good future.

Table 21 *What the unemployed thought the future held for them on Teesside*

No future	12%
Limited future	70%
Good future	17%
Very good future	1%

Table 22 *What the unemployed thought the future held for their children on Teesside*

No future	27%
Limited future	50%
Good future	21%
Very good future	1%

Case study

Les Hill is a 32-year-old crane driver. He lives with his wife Elaine and four children on a council estate in Middlesbrough, where more than one man in three was out of a job when Smith's Dock closed. Les and Elaine married young. He was 18 and she was 16. They have four children.

Les worked at Smith's Dock for 10 years. Before that, he had had short spells out of work. The longest was four months: 'I was climbing the walls.' When the closure was announced, those who wanted to leave early were generally allowed to go. Les took this

option, believing that it would get him a better place in the jobs queue
than if he waited for the final closure.

   In the event, all it got him was a few extra months on the dole. Les
left the yard in October 1986. When it finally closed four months
later, he still had not found work. Like many of the workforce, he
complains that the pay at Smith's Dock was poor, and that on a 'flat
week' (when there was no overtime), he took home less than he was to
receive in benefit. As he put it in April 1987:

> Believe it or not, we're better off. A lot of people might be surprised
> by that. But when I was at Smith's Dock, for a flat week, I was
> getting £96 a week. Now when you work all the rent out, and that
> we don't pay rent with us being on the dole in a council house, it
> works out that we've got three pound more. We're three pound
> better off. So the financial part doesn't really matter.

What did matter for Les were the non-financial benefits of being in
work: the fact that it gave him an aim in life, a structure to the day, a
foundation for self-respect. In common with many of those made
redundant from Smith's Dock, Les threw himself into do-it-yourself
projects around the house. It made sense for two reasons. It is an
intelligent way to invest redundancy money, and it mops up the
sudden, dubious bonus of free time handed out with the severance
cheque. It staves off the feeling that there is nothing to do, and,
hopefully, keeps up morale. In Les's case, though, the strategy was
not completely successful.

> I've never had as much time to myself in my life, and it's very hard
> to fill all your time in. At the moment, I'm working on the house, so
> that's taking a lot of time up, but you need something else. You
> need a routine as I had down at Smith's Dock. I'd worked there for
> 10 years, and you get stuck into a routine, and when that goes, you
> miss it.
>   I've been working on the kitchen. Your mind's occupied, you're
> working away there, and then you come in here and sit down, and
> then I suddenly realise that after I've finished this job, I've got a few
> more jobs to do, but after that, what do I do then? Do I just sit
> around, and wait and see what happens?
>   At the moment, I've plenty to do in the house, but that will
> eventually run out, and I'll be getting up and having absolutely
> nothing to do. You need a routine and something to look forward

to. At the moment I've nothing to get out of bed for, because I
could start the job any time I want.

I watch a lot of television. Go down the club and play snooker,
and that's about it. Mess about in the garden. Clean up, you know.
Not that I've got a good garden, but I dare say it will be, because I
can't really see in the future me getting another job.

Those were Les's thoughts in April 1987. By the summer, when he
had been out of work for nine months, it was clear that he was losing
the battle to keep body and mind occupied, and that, as the list of
home improvements he had to do dwindled, he was becoming more
and more a prey to depression.

You have your days when you get up in the morning, and you
think, 'Oh God, you know, nothing to do again.' But you sort of
snap out of it sometimes, and sometimes you can't, and your day
goes on, and it's a total waste of a day. You get to the point where
you think, 'I can't be bloody bothered', and you sit down. But our
lass, I think she's really been the strongest part of it. She's been the
strength to keep me going. I mean I sit down, and she'll say, 'What
are you going to do today? Are you going to do any decorating
today?'

I'll say 'no'. But she'll sort of keep on at me all the time. And you
feel like saying – you know, but once you get up, once you actually
pick that paintbrush up and start painting, well, after a while, you
get into it.

For Les, the worst thing about being on the dole was the way that
the landmarks of time at work and time at home disappeared, leaving
a featureless landscape where weekdays, weekends, and holidays all
merge into one. He had been a very enthusiastic snooker player, but
now he found even his leisure activities poisoned by the loss of the
working routine. Far from discovering that his increased free time
has allowed him to develop his interest in the sport even more, he
found instead that it is actually destroying his enjoyment of it.

My attitude to snooker is totally different to what it used to be.
Before, when I was at work, snooker was part of my routine. There
was a certain time I could do things. Now there's no job, there's no
routine. I can play snooker any time I want. So it takes the interest
away from the snooker part of my life. I love the sport, but I think
my situation's changed now so that I can't think about it, or play

the sport as much as I used to, because I have so many other things to think about, and the priority is getting another job.

Unemployment was not just an experience undergone by Les. It affected the whole family. From the knowledge of Les accumulated over 13 years of marriage, Elaine had to judge when to comfort and support him, and when to just leave him alone, all at a time when she faced another unwelcome change. Elaine had never been out to work. The home was her territory. Now she found it invaded every day by an unfamiliar intruder.

I'm really used to being on my own. He's round me all the time looking to see if he can do anything for me. He tries but he just gets in the way more often than not. And he has bouts of depression that's hard to cope with. I just have to ignore him and hope that he comes out of it. It just sinks into him every now and again. Sometimes it takes nothing at all to set him off. You just daren't talk to him because he'll snap at you, and he just goes and does something to be out of the way.

He gets into moods when he just can't handle anything. He can't cope at all, and you have to really badger him to do something. You know, with the decorating, he couldn't be bothered half the time, that's why it took so long. But I really got on at him, and in the end he did get round to it. Sometimes, he's just going around all the time saying 'I'm bored, there's nothing to do, I'm bored.' And I'll say, 'Well, I can't find things for you to do.'

Even so, Elaine saw one advantage for herself in Les's loss of his job – company: 'It's someone to talk to now. Before it was lonely. And if he gets another job, that's something I'll have to cope with again.'

For Les, aimlessness was just one problem of unemployment. His other main preoccupation was loss of self-respect. 'I think the most important thing about work is it gives you self-respect. You know, you've got that dignity. The money to me, it doesn't matter. You can't just go along and sign on the dole and wait for your Giro to come in.'

When he first lost his job, and the children could see that their father no longer went out to work, Les feared that he had lost their respect:

When I first left work, it was funny getting up and being there every morning and taking them to school. It was a strange feeling. I mean obviously they don't stop respecting you, but you think all sorts of things. It's not really right. Nothing really changes, except yourself inside.

Les tried a number of expedients to recreate the routine of work that he had lost. One was decorating the home, another was swimming, which he took up in the summer of 1987.

I'm really into it now. I go every morning, and spend an hour, or sometimes two or three in there. It all depends how busy it gets, and it's quite cheap. It's only five pence to get in. I enjoy it. It gets you out, gives you some sort of routine in life, something to get out of bed for.

There is no doubt that Les took unemployment hard. Neither he nor Elaine could imagine his being happy without a job. Les's experiences may have been coloured by what happened to his father. Les believes unemployment killed him.

My father died six years ago. He'd never been out of work in his life, never been ill, and he got made redundant. He was out of work for a spell, then he got a job at a galvanising plant. It was affecting him rather badly, and the doctor told him that he must pack this job in, or face the consequences. So he packed the job in. And from then on, I believe that's when he started to really deteriorate, and he lost interest in things.

He had a smashing garden, but it wasn't enough. What I believe was he missed the routine of going to work and coming home, and going out for his pint. Gradually his health got worse and worse. He ended up in hospital, and he died. He was a cracker of a bloke. Whenever I'm doing a job, I think of my father looking over me, and saying that's how to do the job properly. He was a perfectionist in whatever he did, but he lost his employment, and that's when things started to go wrong.

By the summer, the financial position had deteriorated too. True, Les was on more money than he got in a 'flat week' at the yard, but at times there had been overtime and weekend working at Smith's Dock, which paid for modest luxuries.

You'd pick your wage up, and you'd think, 'I've got a few bob here, we can get something for the house, or get something for the kids', something that you wouldn't normally be able to afford. We're starting to miss those extra little things now. I don't think the kids are feeling it. I don't think they really realise the situation, but, financially, we are struggling a bit.

If we watch what we're doing we'll be all right. I've always been very conscious about paying bills and how much we would take on, and stuff like that. You had to be when you were down at the dock.

In order to safeguard their financial position, the Hills had used part of Les's redundancy payments to buy the television, instead of renting it, and to pay off a number of HP debts.

His long spell of unemployment did not discourage Les from chasing every job vacancy that appeared on the horizon, however faintly. This meant acting on the most tenuous rumours, like a story that there was labouring work available for a contractor doing some trunk road repairs: 'I heard about it in the club. I got a number to ring, and 'phoned up. A man said, "I'll ring you back", but he never did.'

Searches in the evening paper or visits to the job centre tended to be discouraging.

I didn't really understand how difficult it was to get a job. There's a job centre in Middlesbrough. It's a big one, but there's not a lot in there. You're talking about security guards – £1.60 an hour. Really, not a job that you could sort of settle into, and say, 'That's it.' You go and have a look, but it's like a brick wall. You know what you're going to see when you get there, but you've got to keep on trying.

Not surprisingly, Les tended to rebound in his job search between hope and despair. 'One night I was driving back to Middlesbrough, and I came over the hill, and I saw all these factories laid out in front of me, all lit up. And I thought, "If there's all this work going on, why can't I get a job?"' On other occasions, the mood is blacker. 'I'll never be out of a job, because the dole office will never shut. That's my job – going down there.'

During his time out of work, Les had brushes with those government schemes designed in the view of some to help the unemployed back to work, and in the view of others to massage the unemployment figures in a downwards direction. Schemes like the Community Programme, or Re-start, were advertised as a way to help the long-term unemployed find their way back into the labour market. Les found the encounters baffling and depressing.

I went to see about a job that was advertised in the *Evening Gazette*. It was a selection of jobs from the job centre, and this one was for a traffic supervisor. There wasn't a lot to the job. You had to know a little bit about motor vehicles and road regulations. I thought 'I'll have a chat about this, it sounds pretty interesting.' The money wasn't fantastic, but it was a job, and it sounded like something I could do. So next morning I went down to the job centre, and went up to the lad behind the desk, and said I was interested in this job.

He went off and got the card, sat down, and told me about the job, and asked me how long I'd been unemployed. I said 'Well I've been unemployed since October', which is nine months. And he said, 'I'm sorry, but you can't go for this job.' I said, 'Why not?' He said, 'Well, you haven't been unemployed long enough.'

I said, 'I have.' He said, 'Well no, you've got to be unemployed 12 months.' I said, 'Why's that, then?' He said, 'It's a Community Programme job, and the rules stipulate that you must be unemployed 12 months.' He said, 'But if you come back in three months' time, the job'll probably still be there.' So that's when I sort of lost my cool a bit. I said, 'Well, if it's going to be here in three months' time, why can't I have it now?'

Anyway, off I went back home again, and the same thing every night, looking in the situations vacant. And one morning I had a letter through the post, and it was from the Manpower Services. And I thought, 'Well, something's starting to happen!' So I read it, and it's a smashing letter. It's from the Re-start people, but it said in one place, 'Re-start is for people who've been unemployed for a long time.' That got me, because I had already been told two weeks beforehand that I hadn't been unemployed long enough.

Anyway, I keep on going, and it's a date for an interview next month. And right at the bottom, it says, 'Please let me know if you cannot come, because under the benefits office rules, people who do not attend interviews without good cause may lose their benefit.' So it was a nice letter, but at the end there was a threat, saying that if you don't come, if you don't give them a good enough reason, that my kids are going to suffer. And I've never been out of work in my life, and I'm getting letters sent like this.

So I was straight on the 'phone to the job centre. They said, 'Would you like to come down on Monday?', which brought the interview forward actually. I said, 'Yes, I'll come down this afternoon, if you like.' So on Monday, I went down, and I think it was the manager I spoke to. He gave me a lot of promises, saying 'If you come here, we can put you on a training course.' But then I countered that by saying, 'If, for instance, I wanted a course in joinery, would you put me in for it?' He said, 'Certainly.' I said, 'Right, at the end of that I'd get a City and Guilds?' He said, 'Yes, if you pass.'

I said, 'Well, what good would that be to me?' He said, 'It would improve your job prospects.' I said, 'A lot of firms won't entertain people like that.' Tradesmen, they have to go through an apprenticeship of so many years, but somebody going on a course, they only do it for a few months. You can understand the tradesmen objecting. Why should any Tom, Dick or Harry just come straight into their trade, and take away their opportunity for a job?

Les's view reflects a widely held scepticism on Teesside about training courses. In a highly competitive job market, the argument goes, what use is a crash training course? Employers can pick and choose, so surely they are going to choose the man who has served a full apprenticeship, and picked up years of experience on the job? 'I don't really see the point in all this training, because there's plenty of tradesmen in this area that've been made redundant, and yet they want to make more tradesmen. Just sort of giving them a City and Guilds, and "There, go on your way." '

As he faced the prospect of an ever-lengthening spell of unemployment, Les was in a dilemma. It was his profound unhappiness and discontent about being out of work that kept him searching so determinedly for a job. Yet, for the sake of his own peace of mind and his relationship with Elaine, perhaps he needed to overcome these feelings. But if he did, would he lose the will to find work?

I think when I was first unemployed, I was living in the past. Years ago, you could just go down to British Steel, knock on the window, and say 'Any vacancy?' They'd say yes or no. If they'd got any vacancies, you could start on Monday. But that's not really the situation now. They're losing jobs all the time. We're losing industry all the time, so the whole situation's changed, and the sooner I face up to it, which I'm starting to do now, the better it'll be all round. I don't know whether it'll help me with that outlook to get a job, but that's the situation. Times have changed, and they've changed so radically that you must adapt. If you don't adapt, you're just going to get left in the dark.

Elaine, though, saw little evidence that Les's attitude had changed, or that he had begun to accept unemployment. 'I don't think he has, no. Maybe sometimes, but when the mood hits him, he's really depressed.' So how important to Elaine was it that Les should get another job? 'It's important to me because of the way he feels about not having a job. It's him that's the importance. I'd like him to be happy again.'

Les increasingly saw his own predicament as part of a wider industrial tragedy being played out on Teesside.

It's devastating really what's happened in Middlesbrough in the last five years. They're closing places down all the time. Where there was all these factories, now there's grass and daffodils shooting up all over the place. I would personally like to see dust and grime flying about and men going to work, and not walking around the town pushing bloody prams, and doing shopping with the wife. That's not the way for a man to live. The way for a man to live is to go out and earn the money.

In the autumn of 1987, Les's hopes were focused on a training course which would provide him, if he was successful, with a heavy goods vehicle class one driving licence. His relentless scouring of the situations vacant column in the local newspaper had convinced him that this was a sector of the labour market where there were vacancies. In addition to going to the lessons, he also got out instruction books from the library. Each night Elaine would test him on the theory of driving.

I know it's a very difficult test, there's a lot to it, but I've got a book from the library, and I'm swotting away on that. I think I've got the ability to handle one of these units, and if I pass, there's quite a lot of jobs going for heavy goods drivers, so hopefully I'll get a job with one of these firms. But if I fail the test, which is quite possible, a lot of people have failed it, I'll be back to BSEL again to go in for another course.

In the winter of 1987, I went back to interview Les and Elaine again to find out whether the hopes of the summer had borne fruit in the winter. By now, it was 14 months since Les had lost his job at Smith's Dock.

When my heavy goods vehicle course was coming up, I was really looking forward to it, because I thought 'Well, this is my chance, I get through this, and here we go, sort of thing.' Anyway, it came up, and I did my course, and I passed. And I came out of that with a class one licence, and I thought: 'Well, the floodgates are going to open now,' and I was on the 'phone the Monday morning, and I got the same story from every single haulage company that I 'phoned up – that they needed me to have two years' experience at least, before they could entertain me.

It wasn't them, it was the insurance companies that required that, and obviously I couldn't say, 'Well, yes, I've got two years, I've done the business', because they might put me on a big unit now, and I might get lost somewhere. They couldn't take that chance on someone that's just started with their heavy goods. So there you've got a sticking point straight away. I was over the moon when I passed, but when I found the facts out, I was gutted – totally, absolutely gutted.

I was way down again. When my course started, I was aiming to get my class one licence, which allowed me to drive any vehicle, but it just wasn't there, the opportunities are not there. It's a bit of a stalemate actually. I'm at the stage where I've got my HGV, and I need experience, but nobody's willing to give me the chance to get that experience. So I don't really know what the future will hold, but what else can you do? Crane driving, labouring? There's just not the jobs around, so it's pretty sick at the moment

I love this town, Middlesbrough, and I wouldn't want to leave it, because for one thing you're uprooting your kids, you're leaving your mates and friends and everything, and you've got to start again. I believe Middlesbrough has a future. There's new firms coming into the area, but it's a very slow process, and there's that many people out of work. But hopefully when the kids come out of school there'll be work for them, or some sort of opportunity for work experience, or something. But I am worried, I think it's natural. I think everybody's the same.

Me being out of work's had no effect on the kids whatsoever. The eldest one, if she's looking a bit down, we find out what's the matter with her if, say, I've been a bit offhand – because you get very depressed and that, and I don't want to let my feelings affect the kids.

Obviously, some days you get up in the morning, and you think, 'Oh, what's the bloody point?', but we always make sure the kids are OK. Elaine, she's coped really well. I don't really think she understands how much it's affected me, because she's still doing exactly the same job as she was from day one. The problem is that she's got me under her feet all the time, and so, if it's affected anyone, it's affected Elaine, but she's coped very well. If I've got on her nerves, she tells me, and that's the end of it.

The conversation was taking place a week before Christmas 1987, and, naturally, dealing with the costs of its celebration was a major preoccupation.

Previous Christmases have been a routine really. You save so much money up, say, six months before Christmas, you put it away, and, by the time Christmas comes along, you've got everything sorted out. Last Christmas was OK, because I still had a bit of redundancy money left, but this year we never really thought about Christmas until it hit us in the face. So we've had to keep a little bit back from the unemployment benefit, and we've managed to give the kids a few things, but it's been a struggle.

Even after more than a year on the dole, Les's emotions were still in conflict, while he recognised that, for his peace of mind, he was going to have to accept being unemployed, he was afraid that if he did so, he would lose his motivation to find work.

I used to get really down sometimes. I'd go out for walks just to try to get away from it, and clear your head a bit, but now I've accepted the situation. I know that it's pointless punishing yourself and punishing your family, so I'll just see what turns up. I used to get really depressed, until my heavy goods course came up, and then that brought a new thing into my life, and it was interesting, and I got what I was aiming for. I got my licence, but then it was back to square one again.

I'm just sort of stationery at the moment. I'm not doing anything. If a job comes up in the paper, I'll write and apply for it, whether it be driving or any job really. I've done as much as I possibly can. I've been to job centres, passed my heavy goods vehicle, I've tried for loads of different jobs. I'll keep on trying because it's the only way to be, or you just lie down and accept it, but I've no intention of accepting the situation.

It's opened my mind up a bit to the way life really is. When I was in work, I thought it was simple to get a job, because I never used to look in the situations vacant columns of the *Gazette*, I'd just fly past that. But now I'm looking in it, and there's nothing there.

When I was at Smith's Dock, I used to think that people on the dole just didn't want to work. That they were too idle, or they were just quite happy with the situation as it was. They were getting enough money on the dole, and they were managing. But now I've been out of work for a year, I realise that that is not the case, because people who want to work, just can't work, because there is no jobs to be had.

For Elaine, the basic problems remained much the same.

Les is more serious. He gets depressed a lot, and I used to try every way I could think of to get him out of it, but I just can't. So I just leave him alone, and he comes round himself. More often than not, I end up getting blamed anyway. It's just someone to let it out on, and he takes it out on me sometimes. He's short tempered. When he was at work, he was quite easy to live with.

When he first started looking for a job, I kept saying to him, 'You're not trying hard enough', and we had a few arguments over that, because he was trying, but I kept trying to push him a bit more. I kept saying 'You haven't tried here', or 'You haven't tried there', and he'd say. 'I have, I have.' To satisfy me, he tried a couple more places. He'd get the same old answer.

So he said to me, 'Get ready, and you can come down the job centre with me.' So I went to the job centre, and there was about three heavy goods drivers' jobs. They all had to have experience, and he'd only had his licence about a couple of weeks then. We came out of the job centre, and he said, 'Now you know what I go through.' And when I came out of the job centre, I felt the hope had gone, because, I thought, 'There's nothing.'

But each time I hear something, I keep saying to him, 'Try that, go in for that' – but you just can't keep on doing it all the time. Sometimes you feel there's nothing there at all, but then there are times if he goes on the 'phone, and he's longer than a minute, I keep thinking, 'He's got one, they're interested', or 'He's got an interview.' But he doesn't even get to the interview stage. They just say 'We have no vacancies', and put the 'phone down. And he goes into a sort of depression after he's had that answer on the 'phone. It must be bad like, going on the 'phone all the time, getting the same answer off a lot of people. It must be really bad. He can't try any harder; he's trying all the time.

Last Christmas, the kids got lots of things for Christmas. We went out a few times. This Christmas, I don't know if we'll be getting out, and the kids have only got a few things. They've got enough, but they've got a lot less than they had last year.

The future's all based on hope. Up until now I don't really see any way out; any way out at all. I haven't really thought about the children's future. The girls I think'll be all right. I'm just glad we haven't got more than one boy.

In February 1988, Les got a job, driving heavy goods vehicles for a contractor on the big British Steel site on the outskirts of Middlesbrough. The hours were long, sometimes as many as 84 a week, but Les was delighted.

It's great. It's marvellous. You seem to have an aim in life. You're not getting out of bed and wondering what you're going to do. You've got a routine. Elaine says she misses me around the house. I was around her for over a year, and she got used to me being round the house, but she'd rather have me back at work. She's very happy.

Elaine said:

Les is happier. He's a lot more contented now. He's coming home and he's in a good mood, where he used to sit moody before. It's a lot more boring. I do my housework and I try to go out for the rest of the day. I've started going to 'keep fit' to pass the time away. The long hours don't really bother me. As long as he's happy, that's all that matters. He just couldn't cope with unemployment at all. He loves work, always has done. It's life itself to him. Work is life.

CHAPTER 6

FILLING IN THE DAY

What a long, boring day.
(Josie O'Marra)

As we saw in the previous chapter, boredom was a major problem for some of the unemployed. In this chapter we will be concerned with how they tried to conquer it, and fill up the long days without formal work.

One way was simply by sleeping. Prolonged periods of unemployment often produce a growing lethargy. In order to try to measure this, we asked our sample at regular intervals whether they were sleeping 'more' or 'less'. In the late spring and summer of 1987, the proportion of unemployed saying they were sleeping more was considerably greater than the proportion saying they were sleeping less. The gap declined as time went on, but in the summer of 1988, it was still apparent.

Some of the increase in hours of sleep might be attributed to people's simply not having to get up early to go to work, or to their taking a well-earned rest after years of hard manual labour. Equally, others might find that enforced idleness led to difficulty in getting to sleep, or some of the decrease in sleeping time might be caused by people worrying more. None the less, the contrast is quite striking and does seem to suggest that there was a growing listlessness among the unemployed, particularly in the early months.

Among the employed on the other hand, there was little difference in sleeping patterns in the early part of the study. Beginning in the winter of 1987, though, there was a significant predominance of 'sleeping less' over 'sleeping more'. It may be that this reflects the growing number of people taking on jobs with very long working hours, or perhaps even a tendency to lose sleep because of worry about the insecurity of jobs.

Table 23 *People's sleeping patterns*

	Sleeping more		Sleeping less	
	Employed (%)	Unemployed (%)	Employed (%)	Unemployed (%)
Round 3	5	39	4	14
Round 4	0	35	0	23
Round 6	4	16	11	16
Round 7	9	15	15	9

We also tried to find out whether the need to fill in the day would lead a predominantly male workforce to take on more housework. This, of course, is an area where people's own perception of how much they are doing may often be at odds with that of other people. This was illustrated by the results of our first round of interviews in the winter of 1986/87. We asked our interviewees if they were doing more of certain household tasks. The answer was that generally they were, with answers ranging from just under 40 per cent saying they were doing more shopping to more than half saying they were spending more time looking after children.

However, when we asked their partners whether they were doing *less* of the same tasks, a rather different picture emerged. In none of the jobs we chose was the percentage of partners doing less anywhere near as high as the proportion of interviewees who said they were doing more. It is possible that in cases where the interviewee had lost his job, there was actually more housework to be done, because of there being another person around the house, but it is hard to resist the conclusion that, at least in part, the men in the survey believed they were contributing a great deal more to the running of the household than their partners did.

When we returned to the question in the spring of 1987, again very substantial numbers of the unemployed said they were doing more around the house. On this occasion we asked partners or spouses who were present whether they agreed with the answers given. In the overwhelming majority of cases (94 per cent), they said they did, though it is not clear how important a wish to preserve domestic harmony was in influencing this answer.

Still, of those who said they were doing more around the house, 30 per cent said they enjoyed it, or that it helped them get through the day, 46 per cent said they did not mind the change, and only 6 per cent disliked or hated it.

Table 24 *Time spent on household jobs (round 1)*

	Interviewee		Partner	
	Less (%)	More (%)	Less (%)	More (%)
Looking after children	2	55	19	11
Preparing meals	4	41	26	15
Housework	2	44	26	9
Shopping	8	39	17	9

Table 25 *Percentage of unemployed saying they spent more time on various household activities (round 3)*

Cleaning	47
Food shopping	39
Cooking	39
Looking after children	36
Washing	21
Ironing	9

Most of the help that is offered to the unemployed is designed to get them back to work, rather than to help make being without a job more bearable. None the less, at the time when Smith's Dock closed, efforts were being made by the local authorities and others in the community on Teesside to provide special services for the unemployed. These included cheap bus fares and reduced entrance fees for swimming pools and cinemas. At the time of the closure, however, only 20 per cent of the unemployed in our sample had heard of these concessions, and still fewer, only 7 per cent, actually took advantage of them.

Along with this ignorance of the few palliatives that were available went an apparent sense of resignation. When we asked the unemployed what facilities could be provided to make life on the dole more bearable, 15 per cent said they did not know, and a further 30 per cent said they could not think of anything. The only suggestion to achieve any sizeable support, from 9 per cent, was for more cheap, or free, sports facilities.

Fifty-six per cent of those without work were members of a church, club or group, but more than 60 per cent of those said they had not found it to be supportive. In addition, 51 per cent said employed members of the community had not been supportive, while 40 per cent said that they had been.

In the summer of 1988, to get more information about how unemployed people *did* fill in their days, we asked them to complete a diary for us in which they set out their daily routine. We asked employed members of the sample to do the same.

Altogether, 83 people completed these diaries. However, the response rate from the unemployed was particularly high, at more than 75 per cent. As you might expect, low or nil cost activities tended to feature more extensively in the diaries kept by the unemployed. For example, the unemployed mentioned gardening, and visits to parents, children and relatives more, especially during the week.

As we have already seen, do-it-yourself materials absorbed a fair amount of people's redundancy pay-outs. The attraction was that they were not only an investment, in that they enabled value to be added to property, but they were also a way of using up time. While both employed and unemployed mentioned decorating or do-it-yourself, the percentage among the unemployed was a good deal higher.

The degree to which the unemployed had to give up their mobility was illustrated by the small number who mentioned going out for a drive. The home-based activity mentioned most frequently was watching television or videos. It actually featured more in the diaries kept by the employed than in those of the unemployed. Both employed and unemployed mentioned sport or exercise, with a slight predominance for the employed, but the one form of exercise that costs nothing – walking – was five times more likely to be mentioned by the unemployed than by the employed.

We know how difficult it was for many unemployed people to fill their days, so it was sad to note that only one mentioned being involved in formal voluntary work, though far more were involved in informal work – suggesting that here might be a pool of time and enthusiasm for voluntary organisations to tap. One of the unemployed was a local councillor, and the unemployed generally were more likely to mention attending meetings of clubs, unions, or, in his case, the local council.

It should be pointed out that no instructions were issued to the interviewees beyond a request that they should keep a diary. What they decided to record was entirely their own decision. On the evidence of what they wrote, the picture that emerged of life for the unemployed was a routine built around visits to relatives, gardening, do-it-yourself, watching television, and reading, with a little sport and exercise thrown in. On the evidence of the diaries, though, it did not look as though the employed had social lives that were a great deal more active. This may be partly to do with the very long hours that some of them were working (see chapter 11).

Table 26 *How people fill in their days*

	Employed (%)	Unemployed (%)
Meeting friends and family		
Contact with friends during week	12	33
Contact with friends at weekend only	16	15
Contact with extended family during week	18	57
Contact with extended family at weekend only	30	21
Recreational activities		
Watching TV/video tapes	78	66
Sport	49	38
Reading	40	45
DIY/decorating	30	45
Gardening at weekends	30	3
Going for a drive	27	12
Gardening during week	22	66
Walking	8	41
Attending meetings (council, club, etc)	6	18
Dancing	4	6
Formal voluntary work	4	3
Informal voluntary work	4	21

Case study

As we have seen, only 5 per cent of the workers at Smith's Dock were women. The canteen was one of the few areas in which they were heavily represented. Josie O'Marra was a part-time canteen assistant, who worked at the yard for 12 years before she was made redundant in October 1986.

Josie was a widow. Her husband Mike, who had been a crane driver at Smith's Dock, had died in 1982. She was now left with four teenage children, Michael, Stephen, Patricia and Joanne, in her council house at Eston, just over a mile from the yard.

Mike wasn't there at the time I started, but my mother-in-law was manageress of the canteen. He was working for a contractor in British Steel, and he got laid off at the Christmas of 1973 because of the coal strike. That's why I got the job.

When I first got married, I worked in a shop, but when you got married there, you had to leave. That was a policy at the time. Then, after I had Michael I worked in a newsagent's. That shut down when it was demolished. Then when Stephen was about

8 weeks old, my mam knew someone who worked in a bingo hall. I
got a job there, taking about £2.50 a week.
    Then when I was pregnant again, I left there, and had Patricia.
My friend next door but one said could I do a relief cleaning job at
the Port Authority. I had a lot of help with baby-sitters, Mike
always worked. I stayed there three years, then I fell with Joanne,
and finished there. And when she was seven months old, I went
down Smith's. That was it.

When Mike died, Josie got a lump sum payment of £16,000, plus a
widow's pension. 'I got all my house done – all the debts I had paid.
Everything brand new in the house right through – all paid for. I took
the kids on a holiday. Generally they just got what they wanted.' She
had the chance to buy their council house, but did not take it. 'I really
regret it now. My rent's £30 a week. I could have had this for £8,000. I
really regret that.'
    From the moment she was made redundant, Josie's expectation
was that she would not find a job. On the day she left in October 1986,
she said: 'There's nothing going for a 42-year-old woman. I expect
people with qualifications to get a job before I would.'
    Josie did not get unemployment benefit, because she had not paid a
full stamp. Her total redundancy pay-out came to £4,000, and, in
addition, she was eligible for a weekly supplement for the two years
after leaving the yard. This was paid to workers over 40, and was
designed to make up their earnings if they were unable to find another
job, or if they took one that was lower paid than their work at Smith's
Dock.
    Josie's entitlement was £20 a week. Out of that, she paid £5.40 tax,
meaning that she received £14.60. She also retained the widow's
pension that she had been drawing while she worked at the yard.

My widow's pension and my family allowance were never affected.
I could get a job with £100 a week, and that would still be all right,
but it was nice on a Thursday evening to walk in with a pay packet.
I was getting £78 a week on top (gross), and I came out with £45-46
depending on the tax. I'd say now I'm about £35 a week worse off.

The redundancy money soon went.

I bought a new suite. The kids got what they wanted, and I went on
a holiday. Before that, I took the kids to Blackpool for five days. It
cost more there than it did for me in Spain. They hadn't had a

holiday since 1983. I took them after their father died. I took them in the October, and went to Spain myself in the April. I'd never been away since '83 really, and I don't suppose I'll be going again. The kids enjoyed Blackpool except for the weather and the gales. That's what cost the money. We had to spend money indoors, on amusement machines and that.

Josie still feels that the money was well spent, though. 'It would have gone just the same. I'd still be in the same position. And I can think now – this time last year, in so many weeks I would have been going to Spain. I can look back on it. The money would have gone just the same, and I couldn't have pinpointed where it went.'
As for the rest of the money – 'I've got a lot of it lent out.' Will she get it back?

I very much doubt it. Four thousand pounds sounds a lot of money, but it isn't. I mean the kids have always been used to getting money off me. Now when I say, 'I can't give you it, I haven't got it', they say 'You must have.' I feel awful because I really haven't got it, and that's it.'
They don't do as much for themselves, that's one thing certain. They accepted it when I was working, especially at Christmas time when we were busy, that I was shattered. They'd help themselves to their tea. They won't move now. They think everything has to be there for them. The lads wouldn't dream of doing anything.

The children have not had a great deal of success in the job market either.

Joanne's 14, she's still at school. Michael's on a Community Programme, which is due to finish about May, so we don't know about him. Stephen's on a Community Programme that lasts till October, and then the same with him. Tricia's still on the YTS till April as a doctor's receptionist, and we think she's going to be kept on.
Michael had a job on a lemonade van when he left school. He'd work from seven in the morning and come back, especially Christmas time, at ten at night. I had to call the police one night wondering where he was. The pay was on bonus. His basic rate was about £30. I think Patricia will be all right, but the two lads, I don't know, there's nothing round here.'

She thinks it is unlikely, though, that they will leave the area.

> You have to have money behind you to go. Stephen tried it once,
> but he was only away 24 hours, because he couldn't get anywhere
> to stay. He went to London. He only had £30, that was all I could
> lend him. Paid his fares and that, but £30's no good in London. I
> went for a few hours myself, and spent that. That was when we
> went on that demo from Smith's Dock. Didn't land there till one,
> we left at six. I still spent £30.

Nor did Josie think that she herself was likely to move. 'I couldn't
do it. I was born here, live here, still got a mother here. Got my sister
and my mother-in-law. And I haven't got a man behind me. Be
different if I was married and everyone was going. That'd be a
different thing altogether.'
For Josie the worst thing about being unemployed was mind-
numbing boredom. For the first year of unemployment, her loneliness was alleviated by having her younger son Stephen at home with
her (they used to go and sign on together), but even that did not dispel
the boredom:

> There's only me and Stephen in the house once they go to work. I
> more or less get up when I feel like it. I can hear them go out at ten
> past eight in the morning. I'm used to being up. I'm not a sleep-in-
> bed. I think, 'Oh, what a long boring day.'
> So when I do get up, I just potter about, and the rest of the time I
> just spend watching television, until it's time to go and do the teas,
> and then I'm back to square one, watching the tele again.

When asked whether she could think of anything that might solve
the problem of her boredom, Josie replied:

> No, there's no way. I don't like just going out shopping to start
> gossiping, I'm not that sort of person. If I've got to go somewhere, I
> just want to go there and get back. What do they call that thing
> when you don't want to go anywhere? Well, that's how it's getting.

Now that everyone else was out of the house all day, the effect on
Josie was even more pronounced.

> You just go up the shop, get back in, teas ready for half past four,
> wash up, then sit down in front of the tele for the night. Spending

my time on my own through the day, it's a routine now. There's
some days I'm glad of somebody to walk in to talk to, and there's
days when I think, 'Oh, I wish they hadn't bothered coming.' It's
horrible. You want somebody, but you don't want them.

With many of those who had been firm friends at the yard, Josie
had now lost touch.

I don't see them much. I don't go anywhere. I just stay in the house.
If anyone wants to come in here to see me, they can, but I'm not one
for visiting. When my son goes down the club, I'll say, 'How's
Marlene been?' or 'Who was in?', just to know that they were still
there, sort of thing.
   I go out of a Friday to the club. A few of the lads go down there.
Some days they do get reminiscing. 'Hey, those sandwiches down
there . . .', just for a laugh. I used to go out more. I could go
whenever I felt like it.

She felt very strongly the contrast with how things were when she
had her job at the yard:

You miss your friends. We used to have laughs, good laughs. And
it's not just that. You get up, they're long days now, and you
sometimes think. 'I'd be doing this at this time, or I'd be doing that
at that time.' We had a set time for everything. You know, like to
have lunches ready for 12. Now we'd be up and about doing about
250–300 dinners.

Josie could not see any escape from her predicament.

I look around, but there's nothing really there. I'm 42 years old, my
age is starting to go against me, plus I'd sooner see Stephen in a job,
and, like, make my family employed. Because I've worked all my
life anyway, but I'd still work, if I could get a job.
   As time goes on, you think 'this is it'. When you're over 40, you
hear, 'Over 40? Don't bother applying.' I know a friend of mine,
she's wrote for loads, she was told, 'If you're over 40, no work.' It's
stupid. I don't know why they think you can't do a job when you're
turned 40. They just think you're useless, you're finished. You
resign yourself to it, I think, about your fifties. 'Time I packed in,
time I gave up.' But when it happens in your forties . . . I just hope
something comes up.

More or less I could only go back to what I've already done, and through the years, I've been through quite a few jobs. I've always worked. I've been a shop assistant, a bingo caller, a barmaid, a cleaner in offices, and a canteen assistant. So, you see, they're my qualifications – that's what I could do.

When it came to looking for a job, Josie found herself rather devoid of ideas in the face of the overwhelming difficulties of the labour market:

I just go round the job centre – mind you, round this area, a lot is if you know somebody that'd speak for you. I mean it happened in years gone by, that's why I got half the jobs I was in – somebody would say: 'Josie, can you do this, can you come and help us out?'

And that's what it is now. It's not what's up in the job centre, it's who people know. They know somebody's leaving a job or just going off for a few month or so. 'Can you fill in?', and that's how it works. You're just filling in, but I'd be willing to do that.

Nor was Josie's bleak view of her employment prospects much modified by a Re-start interview she had attended in August 1987 at Redcar Job Centre.

I went down there, and they asked how long I'd been out of work, and I said since the October before, and they said, 'Oh, I don't think you've been out of work long enough. What do you get?' I said, 'Widow's pension, family allowance.' She said, 'Oh, I don't know whether you should be here or not. You don't really make any difference to us, but I'll have a look.'

She got this book out – Community Programme. She said, 'There's some going to start for older people, but you haven't been out of work for long enough yet.' She said, 'Are you sure you're getting enough money?' I said 'Yes, I think I'm getting everything I'm entitled to.' 'Ah, but you never know', and she tried to 'phone up Eston, but she couldn't get through.

The upshot of this was that Josie visited the benefits office, armed with a letter from the job centre, and was told that she was, indeed, getting all she was entitled to.

It might sound as though Josie's Re-start interview was of very limited value, but that did not prevent her being called for a second one in March 1988. Again, the venue was Redcar. The bus fare was 60 pence each way from Josie's home.

> Whereas before you got your bus fare paid when you went – you gave your name and your travelling expenses, and you got it back. This letter I've got here says that's finished. You get anything over a pound. So I'll be entitled to 20 pence. Fancy standing in a queue to say 'I want twenty pence.' And I don't think anything will come of the interview, anyway.

This conversation was taking place the morning after the 1988 budget. It felt odd to hear that the Government was determined to make Josie pay £1 towards her bus fare to an interview she had not sought, when the day before the Chancellor had handed out £2 billion in tax cuts, much of it to our very richest people.

In common with many unemployed parents, Josie was more concerned about what kind of future Teesside would offer her children, than with what it held in store for her, and the future she saw was bleak:

> I'm dreading it really. Michael's got a job for a year, and after that we don't know. Stephen, we don't know what he's going to do. Tricia, hopefully, she's all right, and Joanne, well, the kid's a good trier at school, but I can't see it's going to be any better in two years' time for her than it has been for them, really.

As for her own chances of getting a job, Josie summed up the hopelessness into which many of our sample had sunk: 'I very much doubt it. Unless a miracle just came to the door, and said, "Do you want this job?", and I'd take it. But I can't see it.'

CHAPTER 7

GOING DOWN WITH HIS SHIPYARD

People feel you're over the hill
by the time you get to 50.
(Roger Spence)

Altogether, there were a dozen people in our sample aged 60 or over, but most showed no wish to end their working lives, and, instead, searched determinedly for jobs. Only three of our interviewees described themselves as 'retired'. We constructed a small questionnaire especially for them to find out whether they had retired willingly, or whether they had, in effect, been forced into it by the depressed labour market on Teesside. Two of the three said they would not have retired if Smith's Dock had remained open, and that they would have worked until the age of 65, though only one said he might accept a job if one was offered to him now.

In fact, most of those in their sixties continued to look for work after the yard closed. 'You sit and think, "I've got five years to go, I need some money, how are we going to live?" ' said one. 'I thought I can work till I'm 65. Men retire at 65. I didn't see any reason why I should have to pack in work at 60.'

Case study

One of those who was nearing the end of his working life when the closure of Smith's Dock was announced was the managing director, Roger Spence. He was aged 56 at the time. He could have taken a job elsewhere in British Shipbuilders, but he decided to go down with his shipyard.

Roger Spence had spent his whole working life at Smith's Dock. When he came, Great Britain was building half the world's ships. By the time he left, our share of the world market was down to 1 per cent. No one at the yard doubted his commitment to its survival as he scoured the world for orders in an ever more desperate search. In the words of one worker – 'He was like a stick of rock, he had Smith's Dock stamped right through him.'

The Spences live in a very pleasant house in a rather exclusive area of the pleasant town of Guisborough, and were sufficiently comfortably off to be spared the material deprivation that affected many of the former workers at the yard. That would not necessarily protect Roger from the psychological consequences of unemployment, though, and in his case there was the burden of responsibility that came from knowing he had been the man in charge of the stricken shipyard.

Speaking four months after the final closure, he said:

I try not to think about it too much now, but when I do, I don't feel any better about it, because it was an excellent establishment with extremely good managers, and, of course, whenever you see something like that disappear, it's very hard, especially as I was in charge of it. Of the 1,400 people or thereabouts, I don't know how many have been able to get jobs, but I suspect quite a lot haven't, and I think their lives must be very difficult, and I don't like that at all either.

I was extremely busy, of course, and suddenly, you know, having been in charge of a large establishment like that, taking a lot of responsibility, you're thrown on to a totally different situation. I can't say that I haven't enjoyed my leisure, though, and I intend to continue to do so. I was supposed to go on until I was 65, but with the pressures that were increasing in the industry, I sometimes wondered if I'd ever make it to that age. In some ways, I think now is a better time to retire if you've got to, rather than taking the flack for another eight or nine years, which is what would have happened. So to that extent, from a personal fitness point of view, I don't mind.

The industry was in a crisis for 10 years before we closed down, and it's something you get used to, but I think the stress none the less on everyone of working in an industry like that was pretty great, and on the people in charge even greater. I've always had a great deal of admiration for our shipbuilders, but it's not shared by our lords and masters apparently. The shipping industry's in a pretty bad shape in this country. Shipping as well as shipbuilding, one thing follows the other, and I don't think the general public realises how bad it really is, and I think that's extremely regrettable, and I think the nation will live to regret it.

When the closure was announced there was a four ship order, of which three were still to be built, and those three ships were built on time and delivered on time. I don't think I can recollect any company doing that sort of thing once a closure's been announced, and that tells you something about the calibre of the people on Teesside that have got a tradition of heavy industry, and the thing I feel really bad about is that that kind of thing is going to disappear, and I don't know what's going to replace it.

So I feel bad especially about the people in the middle of their careers in the industry who have to look for something else at a time when it's very difficult, especially those with families and mortgages and all the usual encumbrances. I'm lucky, you see, because I've finished with all that at my age. And I feel apprehensive about what their children and grandchildren are going to do in the future, because Teesside was always steeped in heavy industry, and that's the declining part.

There might have been two cars, one a Daimler, in the twin garages, but Roger Spence still found himself, like so many of his former workers, signing on the dole.

I don't know whether you call it unemployed. I actually took early retirement, so to that extent, I'm unemployed at the age of 57, and I suppose that's the trend these days. There's a lot of people who believe you're over the hill by the time you get to 50, until they get to 50, and then, of course, they quickly change their minds.

So what was the effect on Roger's self-esteem of the sudden change from boss to jobless. Did he feel rejected?

Oh no, personally I think there's a lot of eyewash talked about that. I may have felt like that had I been 10 years younger. It never occurred to me then that there was any chance, even if there had been, I would have figured I could have gone out and got another job.

I feel, not rejected. I feel as if I still had a lot to contribute to the industry if I'd stayed in it, but, of course, I'm not the only one who's been pitched onto the unemployment market, not by a long chalk, and I don't feel particularly bad about it now unless I hear something about the industry, then I start thinking about it, and I get a bit depressed, but it soon passes.

I've become a sort of painter and decorator and general labourer, and I clean cars and cut grass and paint things. I've got a boat down in Norfolk, so we go boating quite often. My days are full, strangely enough, I'm never bored, and I never have the time where I haven't got something to do. So I sometimes think I had more spare time when I was working than I have now, but, as I've said, I was one of the lucky ones. I was at an age where I could take an early retirement pension, so I've got something to live on. There are a lot of others who were not in that happy position.

The fact that the Spences were financially secure meant that Jean Spence was able to enjoy some of the effects of Roger's losing his job. It may also be that living in a large, comfortable house also played its part in being able to appreciate the liberation from work.

I have welcomed it really. I'm quite surprised how much better life has become now that Roger's at home, even though he does get under my feet sometimes, but it's nice to have a bit of company around the house. He's just the same Roger that he always was, except that he was always asleep. He'd come home and collapse in a chair and go to sleep, and you didn't really see a lot of his personality.

I didn't envisage this at all. I expected it to be going on for several years yet, all this work, and having to amuse myself and find something to do all the time, but I'm very sorry about it all. I feel sure a lot of wives must feel the same, and I think it's a shame when husbands are thrown out of a job, especially the ones with families that have to be brought up. I think it's terrible really, but there is this bonus that husbands are around and I feel sure a lot of wives must feel the same as I do.

Jean, though, was also worried that the charms of a life built solely around the home might eventually pall.

I'm a little bit bothered about boredom setting in later, and I would really like to see us do something positive eventually. At the moment, it's fine just relaxing, and enjoying relaxing as well, but I really do think that something will have to be thought out and prepared for. I would like to start up in some completely different business from shipbuilding. Obviously, there's nothing left in shipbuilding, but I think it would be nice to start something, or for

Roger to take on a part-time job of some kind, which I don't think he's very happy about.

It was not a suggestion that produced any marked enthusiasm from Roger:

Right now, I don't feel the need to at all. I mean 40 years in shipbuilding is like a baptism of fire that goes on forever, and the flack's been increasing to such a degree that I sometimes think only a lunatic could start another business in this day and age, because you're likely to come a cropper. I'm not a gambler and never was, and you might come a cropper, and get an ulcer as well, which seems to me a bit of a stupid thing to do.

So right now I don't think it's a good idea, but, of course, I might change my mind. As Jean said, come the winter or next year, maybe I'll feel like doing something, but just what I don't know. I've always been interested in boats, and I think I might like getting involved in that kind of thing, but in what capacity, who knows? Maybe just cleaning for somebody else, I'm pretty good at cleaning now.

As soon as I retired, I had time to take stock and look round the property, and I suddenly realised that it had suffered from about 10 years of neglect where I hadn't had the time or the energy to do anything much except cut the grass. So a bit at a time, I started to restore the bad paintwork and grotty woodwork and everything else, and that takes up a lot of time, and I actually haven't got as much time to do other things that I'd planned to do, as I thought I would. I've been far too busy to indulge in my boating activities and model-making activities and all that sort of thing, and my jazz that I used to do.

So when Jean said that I'd probably find myself getting bored in a year's time, I don't really think I will because there's lots more things that I used to like to do that I intend to start again, once I've got on top of the care and maintenance project.

CHAPTER 8

MAKING ENDS MEET

We're just surviving.
(Tommy Cushley)

As we have seen, British Shipbuilders estimated that the average redundancy payment at Smith's Dock was between £6,000 and £7,000. The total amount received was made up of a complicated package of the redundancy payment itself, a closure bonus equivalent to 10 weeks' pay, and 13 weeks' money in lieu of notice. Temporary workers were not entitled to all these benefits.

We asked our interviewees how much they had received in total – nearly 90 per cent of our sample were prepared to answer. Almost a third got £5,000 or less – including a small number who said they got nothing. The biggest group were those who received between £5,000 and £8,000, though more than a fifth got more than £10,000, including a handful who were paid more than £14,000.

Table 27 *Redundancy payments received (in pounds)*

	%
Nothing	4
Up to 2,000	11
2,001 – 5,000	16
5,001 – 8,000	36
8,001 – 10,000	11
10,001 – 14,000	17
14,001 – 18,000	3
More than 18,000	1

Note: These figures are based on an 87% response rate.

Not surprisingly, those in work, who had the benefit of a wage coming into the household, were more successful at hanging onto their redundancy money than those out of work, though even among them, more than a quarter said the money had all gone or nearly all gone by the winter of 1987. Six months later, this had risen to more than half. Among the unemployed, the proportion saying that their money had all gone or nearly all gone stayed fairly static at around 60 per cent, but those saying they had a sizeable chunk left (say, 50 per cent or more) dropped by almost half. Those who were sick or retired also saw their nest egg disappearing fairly quickly. The proportion saying the money had all gone or nearly all gone doubled between Christmas 1987 and the summer of 1988, reaching more than 40 per cent. (Incidentally, the increase in the proportion of the employed who said they had all their redundancy money left could be partly explained by the large increase in the total number of people in work, but more probably results from people's inexact calculation of just how much of their redundancy money was left.)

Table 28 *Proportion of redundancy money left*

	Employed		Unemployed		Training or education	Sick or retired	
	Round 6	Round 8	Round 6	Round 8	Round 6*	Round 6	Round 8
	(%)		(%)		(%)	(%)	
All gone	22	40	42	46	18	7	37
Nearly all gone	6	11	17	14	9	14	5
About 25% left	16	6	9	20	37	21	—
About 33% left	3	7	3	—	—	—	11
About 50% left	22	13	6	6	23	14	26
About 75% left	23	14	16	6	9	22	16
100% left	5	9	6	3	4	22	5

* The number in training and education in Round 8 was too small for the figures to be meaningful.

For those claiming benefits, though, there is a powerful disincentive against hanging onto redundancy money. Any substantial savings you have are liable to lead to your benefits being lost or reduced. At the time when the closure was announced, you could not claim supplementary benefit if you had capital of more than £3,000. If you are unemployed or fear you soon may be, therefore, the sensible thing to do is to pay off debts, or buy things you need.

This consideration does appear to have influenced the way our interviewees spent their redundancy money. More than half said they had bought consumer goods or do-it-yourself materials. The next biggest group, comprising more than 40 per cent, said they had invested the money. Other common uses were paying off debts or the mortgage, buying a car or taking a holiday. There were few major differences between how the employed and unemployed had spent the money, except that the unemployed were more likely to have spent it on paying off debts or the mortgage, and the employed more likely to have used it to buy a car.

Table 29 *How interviewees spent their redundancy money*

	%
Consumer goods/DIY	59
Invested it	41
Paid off debts/loans	26
Holidays	26
Motor vehicles	26
On the family	24
On the mortgage	9
Starting a business	3

Note: Interviewees could select more than one category.

Another feature of the redundancy package was what became known as 'make-up pay' – a taxable supplement for those over 40 who could not get a job at all, or who could not get one that paid as well as the job they had had at Smith's Dock. In the spring of 1988, 31 per cent of our sample said they were receiving this payment. Of those, most were getting £30 or less. The highest amount being received was around £70 a week.

Table 30 *Amount of make-up pay (in pounds per week)*

	%
Less than £20	17
About 20	21
About 30	12
About 40	12
About 50	12
51 – 60	19
70	6

No doubt the redundancy money was extremely welcome, because the majority of people in the whole sample, not just the unemployed, consistently said they had less money coming into the household since Smith's Dock closed. By the time we reached the spring of 1988, only 30 per cent of our sample were still out of work, but the majority of interviewees – 62 per cent – still said they had less money coming in since they left the yard. (We shall examine the financial rewards and other aspects of the jobs that people got in chapter 11.) In other words, financial difficulties resulting from the closure were not confined to the unemployed.

Table 31 *Proportion of people who had less money coming into the household*

	%
Round 2	70
Round 3	76
Round 7	62

From the start of the survey, there was always a group of people who had worries about paying the mortgage or other household bills. In the winter of 1986/87, 17 per cent said they were worried about paying the mortgage or rent, and 25 per cent said they were worried about other bills. On two occasions in 1987, we asked the unemployed how far these worries had developed into actual problems in meeting household expenses. On each occasion, there was a substantial minority who reported difficulties in meeting the basic expenses of living.

Table 32 *Proportion of unemployed people who had problems paying household bills*

	Round 2 (%)	Round 4 (%)
Mortgage	7	4
Household bills (e.g. gas, electricity, rent)	13	6
Other expenses (e.g. food)	1	3
Combination	15	13

Among the most spectacular victims of the closure were two interviewees who had their homes repossessed by the building society when they were no longer able to keep up the mortgage payments. Ironically, both men involved had worked since leaving the yard. In one case, the main problem was the change in the benefit rules which came in at the beginning of 1987. Until then, an unemployed owner-occupier had his mortgage interest paid in full by social security. Under the changes, only half the interest payments were to be met during the first 16 weeks of unemployment. Those already receiving benefit stayed on their existing arrangements, so people who went on the dole before January 1987, by which time most of the Smith's Dock workforce had left, would be considerably better off than anyone who went on the dole after then.

As we shall see, this change hit those who had to take temporary or contract work particularly hard. This man was a case in point. He had had four jobs since leaving Smith's Dock.

Every time I went on the dole I got into debt with the mortgage. Then when I got a job again, I got in touch with the building society, and tried to make up the money. Then I got back on the dole again, so the debt got deeper and deeper. And the last job I got, I tried to make up the money again, but I was only on a low wage, and they wouldn't accept the extra amount of money we could afford to pay them on top of the normal mortgage, which was only £20 a month. They wanted £50.

So, in the end, when I lost that final job, that was it. I just told them they could take the house. I didn't fight them for it. I just couldn't go on any longer. It was a mounting debt that I couldn't see me clearing off, unless I found a permanent job, which round here I just couldn't. I've had four jobs since I left Smith's Dock, but if I'd have known then what I know now about the way this benefit's been changed, I'd have gone on the dole from day one of leaving Smith's Dock, and we'd have still been in our house now.

For many people, the effect of this benefit change has not just been hardship, but also a disincentive to work. Unemployed home owners who were getting their mortgage interest paid by social security had to think very carefully about whether it was worth taking a temporary job, if at the end of it, they were going to lose half their mortgage interest payments. The benefits system includes another bizarre disincentive to work. Unemployment benefit is not means-tested. Even a millionaire will get it for the first year he or she is out of work, provided that the relevant stamps have been paid. However, at the time Smith's Dock closed, the rules said that at the end of that year, the claimant would become dependent on supplementary benefit. (If the claimant was entitled to things like mortgage interest and payments for children, he or she would be already claiming it.)

Now supplementary benefit *is* means-tested, and if the unemployed person's spouse or partner is working, everything he or she earns over £4 a week is knocked straight off the supplementary benefit entitlement. Not surprisingly, many take the view that it is not worth working for £4 a week. So, while we found that 16 out of 69 spouses in work had obtained the job since Smith's Dock closed, another 12 spouses had given up a job. Four said it was because of the effect on their husband's benefit.

As we saw in chapter 5, more than 40 per cent of the interviewees found going to the benefit office a depressing experience, but what about the level of benefits received? No less than 76 per cent said that the benefits they were being paid were not enough to live on. When we asked the whole sample what they felt about the level of benefits, 87 per cent agreed that they did not allow people to live adequately. Only 6 per cent disagreed.

This was before the far-reaching and heavily criticised changes in the benefits regulations introduced in the spring of 1988. These involved the abolition of supplementary benefit, and its replacement by income support, and the drastic reduction of one-off grants for things like cookers or furniture, and their replacement by a system in which the claimant would often be given a loan which would have to be repaid out of benefits. Sixteen people reported that these new rules had changed the amount of benefit they were receiving. Two said they were getting more, and 14 said they were getting less.

It was disturbing to note that there was consistently a minority of our sample who said they did not have enough money for food all week. By the spring of 1988, this figure had reached 17 per cent, or 30 people. The most common response was to borrow, usually from friends or family. Nine did this. Three said they spent less on things like children's clothes or shoes. Two said they were using up their savings, and four said they and their partner sometimes went without food so they could feed the children.

We looked at the question of borrowing in more detail. Altogether, 18 per cent of the sample said they had had to borrow to meet some of their living expenses. The things for which they needed the money included the mortgage or the rates, bills, food, and children's clothes and nappies. One interviewee reported borrowing money and getting food from the church at Christmas 1987, when his contract job ended, and he could get no help from the DHSS for two or three weeks. The majority of those who had to borrow said they felt guilty, degraded or embarrassed. Only two said it did not bother them.

Paying for Christmas proved a particular problem for some of the unemployed, with more than a fifth finding it a struggle, though an equal number enjoyed it. Six described Christmas 1987 as 'terrible' or the 'worst Christmas ever'.

In order to arrive at a picture of overall changes in spending patterns, we asked our interviewees regularly whether they were spending 'more', 'less', or 'the same' on various items. (It is worth noting here that you would normally expect people to be spending 'more' on things as time went on, because of the normal process of inflation.) As far as the unemployed were concerned, the thing that showed the biggest drop was 'saving'. There were never fewer than 60 per cent who said they were saving less, and only a handful said they were saving more.

The other categories where there were big reductions were drinking, entertainment, holidays and clothes. Smoking was reduced too, though not by such a large amount. There were also clear reductions in spending on food, the car, and hire purchase and television rental, probably reflecting the tendency of people to use their redundancy money to pay off debts, or to buy a television instead of renting one.

It was not possible to save on everything, however. A significant proportion of the unemployed regularly told us they were having to spend more on heating, or gas and electricity. This was presumably the unavoidable consequence of having one member of the household at home for more of the time, and must have been a particularly galling extra expense for those forced to depend on state benefits which so many found inadequate.

Among the employed too, there seemed to be reduced spending on some 'luxuries', such as smoking, drinking, hobbies and entertainment – perhaps reflecting the lower pay rates or, perhaps even more important, the insecurity that many experienced in their new jobs. One curious point is that among employed and unemployed, there did seem to be an increase in the amount of money spent on the telephone. Perhaps this reflected the increased use made of it to look for a job.

Table 33 *Spending patterns: percentage of interviewees spending more on various items*

	Round 1		Round 2		Round 3		Round 6		Round 7	
	e	u/e	e	u/e	e	u/e	e	u/e	e	u/e
House	14	8	32	14	25	11	19	13	39	39
Heating	5	26	—	—	9	17	20	31	13	24
Electricity/gas	10	25	14	22	13	20	21	31	13	22
Food	14	11	14	14	26	21	26	18	21	14
Clothing	9	8	23	8	26	13	25	9	29	—
Car	43	8	47	12	39	32	33	13	24	13
Savings	22	8	23	8	26	5	24	3	31	4
Insurance	13	6	23	8	29	9	14	9	15	10
Drinks	—	9	9	5	6	4	13	10	11	6
Smoking	—	5	7	6	5	13	25	21	16	13
Hobbies	9	18	10	23	8	31	20	22	9	18
Entertainment	13	5	5	10	9	5	18	4	10	6
Holidays	13	7	14	9	32	10	18	8	10	7
Children	27	12	21	17	30	24	43	19	39	11
Pets	—	5	—	7	—	5	11	14	12	11
Telephone	24	12	32	11	32	21	42	36	24	23
Hire purchase/ TV rental	17	5	14	7	13	2	17	15	4	8

Note: e = employed; u/e = unemployed

Table 34 *Spending patterns: percentage of interviewees spending less on various items*

	Round 1		Round 2		Round 3		Round 6		Round 7	
	e	u/e	e	u/e	e	u/e	e	u/e	e	u/e
House	9	23	14	24	3	25	9	31	7	14
Heating	5	16	—	—	9	16	3	10	7	16
Electricity/gas	5	10	5	15	3	13	3	7	4	12
Food	14	28	27	22	12	22	11	24	10	29
Clothing	22	52	23	49	11	39	14	50	16	51
Car	10	37	11	35	3	16	10	27	14	39
Savings	26	67	27	62	26	71	44	69	32	69
Insurance	9	14	—	8	3	9	6	10	5	20
Drinks	38	54	32	59	24	46	32	55	25	56
Smoking	20	36	14	28	14	27	19	26	12	38
Hobbies	23	28	15	18	19	14	24	25	18	16
Entertainment	22	49	27	42	17	36	22	45	26	45
Holidays	35	46	14	42	17	40	23	55	33	46
Children	7	13	14	11	10	7	9	19	—	28
Pets	7	3	8	7	9	3	—	10	4	11
Telephone	14	18	5	22	3	17	3	10	9	16
Hire purchase/ TV rental	25	20	29	29	13	12	11	21	16	8

Note: e = employed; u/e = unemployed

Sometimes, just spending less on items was not enough. Eight interviewees told us they had had to sell things to raise money, and others had had to give things up. The items most commonly mentioned as being sold or given up were the car – seven people; and the video – six people. These you might regard as luxuries, though fairly commonplace ones. In addition, however, the washing machine, the fridge and the vacuum cleaner were each mentioned by two people, and one had had to get rid of the cooker.

Case study

When Tommy Cushley tells you his story, you could think you were actually listening to the economic history of Teesside.

Well, I left school in 1972, and I started doing an apprenticeship at Swan Hunter's, Haverton Hill. I was there five years, and – Jack the lad, out of my time, I thought 'I'll get a job anywhere.' So I left there, and I was on the dole for about a year, and during that time, Haverton Hill closed.

Then I went to British Steel, 1975 or 1977, something like that. I

was there three years, and I got made redundant – it was the
MacGregor axe. So I thought, another doldrums, back on the dole.
Then I got a job at RDL. I was only there 13 weeks, and it was
end-of-contract, so back on the dole again, and this time, I was on
it for four years, but by now I was getting used to it, see?
So, when Smith's Dock came along and they gave me six weeks'
work, I thought six weeks is better than nowt. But when I got there,
some of the lads told me that it'd started with six weeks for them
originally, and it ended up being 12 months, or whatever. So I
thought, 'smashing', and Lesley was expecting the little 'un, so I
thought, 'Money coming in the house – regular wage – great.'

Well, I was there about a week to 10 days, and I got the closure
notice. I couldn't believe it, so it seems everywhere I've been,
everywhere's closed. I've been on the dole maybe about six years in
all.

No wonder there is a joke locally that when men see Tommy come
in through the factory gates, they expect their cards at any moment.

Tommy lives with his wife Lesley, and their four young children in
a council house in Billingham. She has nine brothers and sisters, he
has five. Because he was a temporary worker at Smith's Dock – they
felt, said Tommy, like 'second class citizens' – Tommy got no
redundancy payment.

I didn't get any redundancy money, so it was just like a fortnight's
wages, and you don't get no dole for a fortnight. You live off them
wages, and then you're back to your fortnightly giro, but I'm more
or less used to it, because it's happened so often, and you just
knuckle down and do it. But some of the lads that left school and
got redundancy, they'd never been on the dole before, so it's going
to affect them worse, I think.

At least I'm a bit experienced, you might say, but I'd rather not
be obviously, you know, what with four kids, you need as much
money as you can get, but you're a long time dead, you've just got
to knuckle down, and get on with it, and stop whingeing – just get
on with life.

As with so many of those we encountered, the loss of Tommy's job
meant more tension within the family. 'He gets bored a lot now,' says
Lesley, 'he's lazing around a lot. I give him things to do, like
housework and things, and he'll do it if I tell him to, but that's it. He's
under my feet all the time, whereas, when he was at work, I could get a

lot more done myself, but now I have to give him things to do to keep
him occupied.'

Tommy put it this way:

> It's like 24 hours you're with each other all the time. It's a bit much
> obviously. I mean when you're at work eight hours a day, and then
> you come home, you miss the kids – you haven't seen them for
> eight hours. You can all have your tea around the tele. Now the
> kids get under your feet, and you're shouting at them, and you have
> an argument with your missus or whatever, so, in one way, it's
> really bad, but, as I say, you've just got to get on with it. Knuckle
> down.

Tommy's philosophical attitude is a great help in negotiating the
inevitable ups and downs – the spells in and out of work – of a manual
worker's life on Teesside. It crops up again and again, and if wisdom
is born of experience, then Tommy's thoughts on how to survive the
dole are well worth listening too.

> The only recipe there is is just don't whinge, and get on with it. I
> mean, what can you do? The only other way out is maybe divorce
> or separation, or in your grave. There's nothing else you can do,
> apart from keep applying for jobs – sending CVs here, CVs there,
> and just hope one comes along. That's all you can do, really.

The financial impact of the loss of the job at Smith's Dock is clear.
'It's a big difference. Thirty or forty pounds a week difference, easy.
We're just above water now' – Tommy puts his hand underneath his
chin – 'We're just surviving, but we had our shoulders out as well. So,
yes, it's a big difference. Thirty or forty pounds is a lot of money,
isn't it?'

The task of making the reduced family income stretch to cover the
budget falls to Lesley. 'I'm not money-minded at all, me,' says
Tommy, 'I'd rather spend it – live for today. So if I've got money in
my pocket, it's burning a hole. I only want to spend it, so I'm no good
over bills – Lesley does all that, she's great like that.'

If Tommy wants a night out when he is on the dole, there is an
established procedure.

> I get pocket money. No, it's not as bad as that. The wife, she
> doesn't go out much, she has the kids all the time. I'm a male
> chauvinist. If I wanted to go out, and if I want money, Lesley will

give me it, but obviously if there's no money there, if the funds are exhausted, you can't go, simple as that, so you just sit in and watch the tele.

Within the Cushley household, Lesley has established a reputation as a redoutable financial manager. During one of Tommy's previous spells out of work, she even managed to save up the money for a holiday in Spain.

When we get our money, I see what we have to pay out and do that, and put so much for food, and what's left, usually we share. But he gets something more if he wants to go out to his golf or something. I usually give him a bit extra. I say, 'There's a couple of pounds, you can have that.'
  You just have to manage your money. If you can live on your money, you're all right. You just have to see you don't get into too much debt, because then you're paying all your money out, and you've got no money to spend on anything.

Lesley does the shopping with Tommy on what they call 'a dole day', in other words, when the giro comes.

I cut back on the food, because we get two weeks' money at once. So you're cutting back on food, and if the children want any new clothes or anything, they can't get them straight away. We have to save a bit every fortnight to get things like that. You just really have to cut back on everything, and don't get anything you can do without. You just have to manage with what you've got.

As for the effect on their social life, 'We used to go out together on a Sunday,' says Tommy, 'but we can't do that now, because we haven't got the money, and we used to go out Friday night, or go sometimes on Saturday, and it's just now and again now. We stop in a lot more.'
  One of the challenges for those out of work is to find entertainment that fills up the time, at as near nil cost as possible. Tommy finds it in sport. He is a keen golfer – playing when he can afford the couple of pounds it costs the unemployed for a round on the municipal course. Even more important, though, is his football. He plays three times a week:

There's five-a-side Wednesdays, eleven-a-side Saturday afternoons and Sunday mornings, and there's training, so there's quite a lot. I live for football. Obviously, I love the kids, but I love football, I always have done. We've always been a football-minded family. It's very important, because if you get bored during the day, you can always look forward to playing football. Get your boots polished, get your kit ready, go and play five-a-side at night, and have a few beers with the lads.

It keeps an active mind. Otherwise you'll go under. You're a long time dead, so you've just got to knuckle down. I mean there's nothing else to do, is there? Once you've helped the wife hoover up, I mean, you can't hoover up all day. It's not really costing me anything, but it's keeping me happy, keeping me fit, well, fitish.

Tommy felt quite strongly what he saw as his second-class citizenship as a 'temp' – temporary worker – at Smith's Dock. They missed out on redundancy payments, and as they were also excluded from BSEL's sphere of responsibility, they were on their own as far as finding another job was concerned. He is remarkably devoid of bitterness about the closure, though.

I'm not bitter. I mean Smith's Dock gave me a chance to get a job in the first place, so I can't really feel bitter towards them. I mean it's not their fault that the place closed down, is it? There's nothing you can do. Who do you blame? It's just that we seemed to get the backlash. I don't know – you've just got to take the rough with the smooth, and the last couple of years has been rough, so maybe the smooth's on the way, who knows?

Tommy's view of the future too was in keeping with the mood of philosophical realism that pervades his outlook.

We'll be surviving. Definitely surviving, trying to get your head above water. You can't really look very far. All we look for now is the next giro, that's all you can do, you've just got to survive, spread your money out, and just hope something comes round the corner. Never seems to, though.

In the spring of 1987, neither Tommy nor Lesley saw much chance of Tommy's getting a job. 'The chances are not very high,' said Lesley. 'He's tried. He tried for one not so long back, and put a form in, and never heard a thing about it. All the time you just don't hear a thing.'

Tommy agreed:

You just put forms in everywhere, that's all you can do. I think all they do is just file them, put them in the filing cabinet, and you wait a few months, and you 'phone them back, and they say, 'Oh, will you send a CV in?' 'I've already sent one in.' 'Oh, it must be in our files, will you send another one just in case?'

So really I think all they do is they just put them in the bin, because look how many's out of work, so there must be thousands of people sending CV's in. Obviously, they can't file them all, they wouldn't all sit in the office, would they, in a filing cabinet? So I think nowadays it's not what you know, but who you know. Really you've just got to hear about jobs on the grapevine. If someone's well in somewhere, and you know him, he'll put a good word in for you, and that's how most are getting it, if you know what I mean.

This might sound a rather fatalistic attitude, but, in the event, it did not stop Tommy pursuing such possibilities as there were as enthusiastically as the next man. Billingham's shops are all clustered around the town centre, with the Forum Theatre and the ice rink. It is said to be the cheapest place in England to shop, and in among all the shops is the job centre. The Cushleys live within walking distance.

When the kids are on holiday, all six of us'll go down, and pop in there while we're doing our shopping. When the girls are at school, we still go to the square, the four of us, daily to get bread, milk, whatever, and just pop in. It's very handy, it's just like a family outing. You meet people who are out of work who you used to work with, and you can have a bit of talk, and the women get nattering. It's like a social club over the square. Then you just pop in the job centre, and have a look.

I don't go everyday, but sometimes three or four times a week. But it never really helps. It must help some people because not everyone's out of work, but the job I'm looking for in my trade, they're very few and far between. So it's either change your trade or try something different, which is like leaving school and starting again. So usually I go by word of mouth – if my mates are in work somewhere, they'll tell me if there's a job coming up. I find it more effective that way, on the grapevine, as you might say.

Although Tommy was conscientious about regular visits to the job centre, he often found it a depressing experience:

I don't think there's a very good selection, because they're mostly clerical work, or vast experience needed. The latest vacancies, they're more typists, bar staff – there's lots of bar staff. 'Experienced men wanted here – must have experience.' How do you get experience if you don't get chances? They're very helpful people in there, don't get me wrong, but there could be more selection. Some people just go there for something to do. If it's raining, they'll go in there till the rain stops. You find the same cards every day – apart from the latest vacancies, which change every day. It's depressing. You see people in there everyday, just mooching around. People pop in, sit around, have a smoke, and read the papers.

But I just go in, have a quick look, and if there's nothing, come straight back out, and sometimes I might just go and enquire about a job. It's a depressing place, but you've got to go in, because that one occasion there might be a job, and if you don't go in that day, you've missed your chance.

So what of other solutions to the family's financial problems, like Lesley's taking a job? She had worked in the past as a barmaid, but when Tommy is out of work, the benefit system is a considerable disincentive, even though he could act as a baby-sitter. The problem is that Tommy did not have enough stamps on his card to get unemployment benefit, so he went straight onto supplementary benefit, with the effect that virtually anything she earns immediately hits his benefit.

I used to work, before I had the last baby, but, at the moment, while he's not working, it's not worth my while. I can earn just four pounds. While he's on the social, that's all I'm allowed to work for. Whatever I earn more than that, they take it off his money. It doesn't go very far, four pound, so I just don't bother. If he was working, then I'd go back to work, if I could get a babysitter.

Another way out for the Cushley family might be for Tommy to find a job away from Teesside. Three of Lesley's brothers work down south, sharing a house near London, but the idea of moving the family home away was something he rejected: 'I wouldn't move the whole family because we're settled, the whole family's round Billingham, all the relations, aunts, uncles, cousins, nephews, we're a stone's throw from each other's houses, so moving away would be too much of a wrench family wise.'

Lesley agreed, but felt there was another possibility, that Tommy could go away to work, while she and the children stayed on Teesside:

We wouldn't like to get up and move away, because as he says the schools are here; the kids they like their cousins, they all go to the same school, so I don't think they'd like to move, but I wouldn't mind him going away. It's just finding the work, and then getting back. Sometimes it's too expensive to get back all the time, you might as well stay up there.

Tommy, as the one who would be doing the shuttling back and forth between home and work, was less convinced:

I'd work away, like four weeks away and a couple of weeks at home, smashing. Then it's like a holiday when you come home, but some people work away, and they go home for the weekend, and then they're back. So they don't get much time with the family, and, obviously, I'd miss the family, what with four little 'uns.

What's a weekend? By the time you've travelled, you've got 48 hours. I mean you're probably just getting 24 to 30 hours. It's not much. But I'd definitely work away as long as I could get back and spend some time with the family.

Both Tommy and Lesley were extremely concerned about the future of their children: 'I don't think they've really got a future,' said Lesley, 'not at the moment, but they've got a long time at school yet, so hopefully it might get a lot better in the long term.'

Tommy took a similar view, not because he was depressed about the future of Teesside generally, but because he considered that Britain, as it has evolved, offers little future for working people.

I think the future for children in this area is just as good as anywhere else. The whole country's in a state, isn't it? So everyone's kids have got more or less the same future, unless they're well off, bred into money and that, but working-class people, their kids have all got the same future.

One day, Tommy's endless visits to the job centre paid off. Not that he found a job, but at least he did get a place on a kitchen fitting course at the local skill centre. The course seemed useful: 'I've learned a lot more than I knew before – how to make cabinets, kitchen units, plastering, plumbing, tiling, you name it, lots of things. At the end, you can always go into your own business, can't you?'

Sadly, though, the solution to one problem brought another in its wake. When Tommy went on his course, the Cushleys unexpectedly had their rent rebate reduced; a change, he claimed, which made him worse off on the course than he had been on the dole.

I'm having a bit of bother with my rent. It's like a rebate, and there's about four lads that wrapped in the course, because of finances, you know, they were losing money. Before they didn't pay rent, and now they're having to pay so much. And when I started, they said you wouldn't lose, you'd be better off, if anything. You're allowed 71 pence a day food, and with putting sandwiches up and all that, it's running into more, so we're worse off actually.

Eventually, the Cushleys sorted out their rent rebate, but not before they had had a letter telling them that they were £232 in arrears, and threatening them with court action. While Tommy was on the course, Lesley went back to her old job as a barmaid, and her £30 a week was a useful addition to the £68 a week he was getting on the course. When Tommy finally performed all the abstruse calculations relating to the financial benefits and penalties of the course, he reckoned it left him 15p a week better off.

CHAPTER 9

FIDDLING

If you've got to do it, you've got to do it.

(Former Smith's Dock worker)

The thing that has probably diluted sympathy for the unemployed more than anything else is a widely-held belief that many, if not most, of them are earning money 'on the side' to top up their benefits. Because of the illegality of such activity, it is extremely difficult to come up with any precise figures as to how widespread the practice is, and of what sums are earned in this way.

Estimates of the total amount generated vary widely, from as little as £6 billion a year to as much as £45 billion. If the latter figure were true, however, it would assume that, on average, every household in the country was illicitly earning £40 a week, and equally that every household was spending £40 a week on services provided illicitly.

A variety of phrases are used to describe these activities – including the 'Black Economy', the 'Hidden Economy', or the 'Shadow Economy'. On Teesside, the normal term is just 'fiddling'. I have taken the 'Black Economy' to mean any activity from which people earn money without declaring it to the relevant authorities, whether this be the tax office or the benefit office.

In other words, it is not an activity confined to the unemployed. It could be a case of an unemployed man doing work while still claiming benefit, or it could be someone in employment who also does odd jobs 'on the side' without declaring the income from them, or it could be a self-employed person who does some work 'off the books'. As we have seen, for many of those made redundant at Smith's Dock, the labour market in which they now found themselves was extremely casual and fluid. Someone who suddenly gets the chance of a few days, or a few weeks, work during a spell of unemployment may simply feel it is not worth the potential hassle of informing the benefit office, and then possibly having to sign off, only to sign on again shortly afterwards, with all the disruption to calculation and receipt of benefits that might result, particularly when, as we have seen, confidence in the benefits system is not high.

In a situation where more than three quarters of claimants say that benefits are not enough to live on, where 17 per cent of the unemployed say they do not have enough money for food all week, and where a similar number have habitually to borrow to keep going, it would be surprising if some attempts were not made to earn additional money.

However, another, less publicised, feature of the Black Economy is illustrated in the two brief case histories at the end of this chapter. The fact is the unemployed often use it as a way to get started, particularly in jobs where they have no experience. Their lack of qualifications mean that pay is often low, and work extremely irregular and unpredictable. In those circumstances, the employee might consider it is worth taking the job only if benefits are still claimed. Equally, many of the employers who are offering this kind of work have to operate to extremely tight margins, and, in order to minimise their employment costs, are prepared only to employ those workers who will take 'cash in hand'. Some actually encourage their workers to stay on benefits, so that they will be able to pay lower wages.

Similarly, someone who sets up in business on his own will know that in the early months, things will be hard and very little money may be earned. The Government's Enterprise Allowance Scheme offers a support payment of £40 a week for a year to those who come off the dole to set up their own business, but they have to have £1,000 of their own money to invest in the business. Many will have a 'dry run' during which they continue to claim benefits before they are prepared to take the risk of applying for the Enterprise Allowance, investing their money and signing off the dole.

So this is an area in which there appear to be contradictions in Government policy. There is a well-publicised crackdown on 'scroungers' who claim benefits to which they are not entitled (there have been well-publicised cases on Teesside in which people have been charged in very large numbers after investigators 'swooped'.) At the same time, the Government's determination to break down what it calls the 'rigidities' in the labour market has led to casualisation, erosion of union power and the lowering of wages, all of which increase the pressure on employers and employees to work outside the system.

Because of the difficulties in quantifying the Black Economy and people's understandable reluctance to talk about it, we included a series of questions about it, phrased in different ways, in our questionnaires. In the early interviews, for example, we asked a question about money worries, and then asked those who were worried what they were doing to overcome their problems. Another approach was to ask the unemployed whether they were doing anything to maintain their skills. These two approaches produced admissions from four people that they were working in the Black Economy.

By the fourth round of interviews in the summer of 1987, though, 15 per cent of the unemployed – 17 people – said they were doing jobs on the side to help with household expenses. We also asked the unemployed how they thought other people out of work managed to live; 13 per cent said by doing jobs on the side. These higher figures might represent a higher degree of activity in the Black Economy, or they might reflect the fact that, by this stage of the study, the interviewers had won a greater degree of trust from the interviewees.

In another attempt to measure the extent of the Black Economy, a single question on a separate sheet was left with each interviewee, and they were asked to return them in a pre-paid envelope to the Polytechnic. The forms carried no markings that could identify any individual. A hundred and seventeen returned their sheets, and, of these, 11 said they worked in the Black Economy.

In view of the rapport that was built up over a long period of time between interviewers and interviewees, we felt that one of the best ways of achieving an accurate assessment of the extent of the Black Economy was by asking each interviewer to say what proportion of her interviewees she believed had at some time been doing jobs 'on the side'. In the summer of 1988, this yielded an estimate of 12 per cent, and the interviewers' belief was that only about 4 per cent were currently active.

It has sometimes been suggested that the employed are more likely to be involved in the Black Economy than the unemployed, because their skills are more likely to be in demand, and because they have easier access to transport, materials and tools. However, our estimate was that the vast majority of those who had been involved in the Black Economy were unemployed. It may be that the long hours expected from many of those in work effectively prevented them from taking on any other jobs.

We also asked the interviewers to make some estimate of the amount of money that participants in the Black Economy could earn.

Most of the work appeared to be highly irregular – the odd day's
labouring for 'cash in hand'. Rates of pay seemed to be about £20 to
£30 a day. Even more casual activities, like mending a car, or doing
some gardening, might yield as little as £5. There was also the odd
low-value fringe benefit. One man got four free pints of beer in
addition to his £30! Only 1 per cent of the sample were judged to be
earning regular income from an undisclosed source.

Often those who get involved in the Black Economy for these
reasons do so reluctantly, feel guilty about what they are doing, and
are extremely nervous about being caught. Both of the case histories
feature people who were unemployed for a long time, and who
escaped from the dole queue by going first into the Black Economy.
Now both of them earn their own living, without being a burden on
the taxpayer (the reduction of this burden is, of course, the objective
of the crackdown on 'scroungers'). Ironically, if they had not been
prepared to break the law, it is likely that neither would have got the
job they hold today.

Case study 1

All the companies I rang up said they couldn't take me on because I
had no experience, so I thought to myself, 'How the hell am I going
to get experience?' I got this 'phone call, and this man wanted me to
work for a day. I was frightened, but I said, 'Yes, all right.' I was a
bag of nerves at first, but it went great.

I got through the first day and he invited me again. I started with
two days a week and then three, then a week. This was on the
fiddle, and this is how I got back into the rhythm of work again,
which was great because I was getting the experience I needed for
people to be interested in me. I knew it was wrong, but with me, it
wasn't the money.

I was very very conscious of going out of the house at six o'clock
in the morning, wondering, 'Is anybody watching?' Because it's
happened round here, and people have been dropped in it, and
that's mainly what I was worried about. Somebody knocking on
the door and saying: 'Yes, we know you've been working without
telling us, and your benefits have been stopped.' So it was a very
frightening period.

Why didn't I tell them? If I'd told them I was working, they'd
have said, 'Well, who are you working for?' and I'd have said, 'Mr.
So-and-So', and they would have got in touch with him, and the

snowball would have turned into an avalanche, and he would have been in trouble, because that's how his business runs, and that would have been the end of that little episode. It was 'We need so many people this day and we don't need so many tomorrow or the day after that.' So he can't take me on permanently, because he'd be carrying dead wood.

I knew it was going on, you know going in the clubs, and people saying, 'I've got a little job on the fiddle here.' It's rife in this area. Anybody that's got the chance of a fiddle they jump at it. There's a lot of people who are jealous, who'll jump at the chance to drop anybody in it. I think there's a little reward for people if they inform the authorities.

I was very disappointed having to turn to this type of going on, and I thought, 'The only way now is to work like this, and that's not really on', but I mean if you've got to do it, you've got to do it. I enjoyed the money, but with me, it was the experience I needed.

Case study 2

A common way of entering the Black Economy is to set up your own business without signing off the dole. Often, however, this does not lead to the offender enjoying an enormous income. More usually continuing to claim benefits helps him, or her, to make a living from the business which could not be had without them. When the business *is* providing a decent living, the offender often signs off the dole, and leaves the Black Economy.

On the dole, I got £32 a week, and I could earn £60 or £80 in a good week, but good weeks were few and far between. Fiddling allowed me time to get experience and knowledge. Also, the equipment I had wasn't very good, so I was able to use the money I earned to invest in more equipment. Now, on a good week, I can manage maybe £1,200. That's gross. I'd maybe see a third of that after expenses, and most weeks aren't good weeks.

A lot of people get their experience and knowledge by fiddling at first, unless it's passed down to them in the family. I didn't know anything. I was inexperienced. I think the Government could be more helpful to people starting up in business – both money and advice. They give you some help. You can get loans, but you should be able to get grants too. You can't make a living out of it at first, without the dole.

CHAPTER 10

ON A COURSE

If you mention the skill centre,
they don't want to know.
(Ian Dale)

One of the Government's favoured responses to the problem of finding work for those made redundant at Smith's Dock was to re-train them. In many ways, this approach made sense. Shipbuilding was a dying industry, and, as we have seen, many of those who worked at the yard appeared qualified only for jobs in shipbuilding or other contracting manufacturing industries. The question was whether it would be possible to re-train them in any skills that would find them jobs in Teesside's depressed labour market.

Certainly, BSEL, the company set up to help find jobs for the workforce, put a great deal of its effort into interesting people in re-training, and sending them on courses. BSEL had offices at Smith's Dock, where people could report for 'counselling' on their future. When we did our first interviews in the winter of 1986/87, 56 per cent said that they had considered re-training.

By the summer of 1988, 40 per cent of the sample had actually been on a course. (More than a quarter of these had been on more than one course.) In nearly two-thirds of cases they had gone to acquire a new skill. The other courses had been to upgrade existing skills. The most popular courses appear to have been related to welding. Others mentioned included kitchen fitting, bricklaying, heavy goods vehicle driving and computer related courses. In addition, seven people were studying for a degree.

The main motive for going on a course was a belief that it would help to get a job. This was the reason given by more than three quarters of those who re-trained, but it was not the only reason. Ten per cent went on a course simply because it was 'better than the dole'.

Table 35 *Unemployed people on training courses*

	No. of people
Advanced welding	11
Pipe-fitting/welding	7
Kitchen fitting	5
Computer related	5
Heavy goods vehicle driving	4
Bricklaying	4

I spoke to one man in his fifties who went to be trained in kitchen-fitting. He never expected to find a job as a kitchen fitter. His reason for going on the course was that at the end of it, he would be able to go back on unemployment benefit. As we saw earlier, unemployment benefit is a non-means tested benefit, but it lasts for only a year. This man had lost money when his dole ran out, and he had been forced back onto means-tested benefits. Re-training to him was simply a means of re-establishing his entitlement to the dole for another year.

Still, 85 per cent of those who went on a course said they found it useful or very useful, while 12 per cent said that it had not been useful. When it came to the acid test of whether it helped you to find a job, however, the result was rather different. By the summer of 1988, only a third of those who had been on a course said it helped them to find work. Optimism dies hard, though. Of the 60 per cent of the sample who had still not been on a course, more than half said they would like to go on one.

As we have seen, BSEL played a leading role in getting people on courses. (In the spring of 1987, three quarters of those in training told us their courses had been organised by BSEL.) Setting up BSEL was, indeed, the Government's major contribution to helping to find jobs for those made redundant at Smith's Dock. It was charged with a responsibility to all permanent employees of the yard. Its activities were gradually run down at the end of 1987, so, in the autumn, we decided to see how its consumers had rated its performance. Forty-three per cent of the interviewees said they had found BSEL helpful, but 31 per cent said they considered it had not been helpful, while another 14 per cent said they had had no contact with it.

Case study

Ian Dale is a 27-year-old ex-plater. He is married with two children, and has a mortgage on his terraced house in Billingham. He had spent

eight years at Smith's Dock – 'It's a long time.' He was made
redundant from Smith's Dock in October 1986, but this was not his
first experience of losing his job. Before coming to South Bank, he
had been made redundant at the tender age of 18 from the Haverton
Hill shipyard, when it closed in 1978.

I first met Ian on the day he left the yard. With a group of his mates,
he was holding a 'redundancy party' in the local pub – a brief
lunchtime drowning of sorrows for those who were leaving that day.
The drowning was pretty ineffective in Ian's case; he was extremely
downcast. He had got himself a place on a six-month bricklaying
course organised by BSEL – 'There's not much else I can do.' The
course would be at the local skill centre in Billingham, but Ian did not
see it as the passport to a job. When I asked him how confident he was
that the course would help to get him work, he replied – 'not very
confident really'.

For Ian, working at Smith's Dock had not been a bed of roses. He
had once been awarded £600 compensation after being hit by a piece
of metal when a pulley broke. 'I was glad to get out. I'd had a few
accidents.' Nor was he very enthusiastic about plating as a trade. 'It's
dirty work, you never know what you're breathing in.' He was soon
to discover, though, that regarding the job you had lost as dangerous
or unpleasant was no protection against the depressive effects of
being thrown out of work.

Ian spent three months on the dole before beginning his course,
and when he had nearly finished it, I asked whether he now felt any
more confident about getting a job with this new qualification behind
him. His views had not changed, 'The course, it's OK, but I don't
think it's going to do me a lot of good at the end of the day. I've been
told there's a 50 per cent job ratio for bricklayers. That's 50 per
cent get jobs. So – one in two chances haven't I? Just see what
happens.'

Ian is rather laconic by nature, and deeply pessimistic, some would
say realistic, about his, and Cleveland's, prospects. His own he
summed up fairly succinctly. At the end of the course, he would be
'back on the dole'. Did he expect he would ever work as a bricklayer?
'I can hope I suppose, but I don't know. Just see what happens.'

In fact, Ian found himself putting most of his effort into looking for
a job that would use the skills of the old shipyard trade he had wanted
to escape from – plating, rather than those of bricklaying, newly
acquired at the skill centre. But he was not even optimistic about
getting a plating job. 'In Cleveland, we're top of the unemployment
league, aren't we? I've been trying writing for jobs for my old trade,

plating, and there's nothing. A couple of interviews, but that's it. No light at the end of the tunnel.'

Ian had tried to explore other re-training possibilities when he left the yard: 'He was talking about computers', said his wife Linda, 'that's something he would like to do, but he couldn't get the backing.' Ian took up the story: 'I couldn't get the backing from BSEL. There's a course at this skill centre, where I am now. That's something I really wanted to do, but I just had to let it go. I just had to drop it, otherwise the only way I could have done it was to pay for it myself, and that was far too expensive.'

The value of the course to Ian was twofold. First it was better than being on the dole in financial terms, though he still needed supplementary benefit to augment the £64 a week he was getting, and second, it might enable him to do jobs around the house. As he and his wife Linda were having to launch into some major home improvements, this could be a significant benefit. 'For my personal use, it's a lot of value, but as far as prospects for a job go, I don't know. I'll just have to wait and see. I'm not very enthusiastic.' In the event, he was able to build a fireplace, but for more fundamental work, they still had to call in the professionals.

'I went on the course mainly for my own benefit, so that I can do jobs in the house. If I'm willing to work away – leave my wife, yes, the course will probably have helped me, but I'm not leaving my wife.' The idea of trying to move the whole family was, in Ian's view, quite unrealistic: 'It's a big problem, isn't it, with house prices? I couldn't afford to buy a house anywhere else, and I certainly wouldn't want to rent a house again, not after having my own home.'

Linda was equally adamant that she did not want him to work away from home: 'There's just nothing here for him to do. We don't want to split up – and him go down south, so it's something we've got to put up with.' The closure of the yard had shattered a number of Ian's cherished domestic dreams.

I can't do the things I want to do anymore. I was hoping to sell this house. I had it up for sale, but I had to take it down as soon as I found out the shipyard was closing. We were hoping to emigrate to Australia before they closed down. We were hoping for all sorts of things. It's finished now.

Predictably, the closure and the resulting financial pressures had put some strain on Ian and Linda's marriage: 'It's put a bit of strain on the marriage, we have our little tiffs, don't we.' 'It's always about

money, isn't it?', says Linda. 'About money, yes. If there's any strain
whatsoever, it's about money.'

In the early days after Ian lost his job, things were not too bad,
thanks largely to the redundancy pay-out of £8,000.

> Things were OK then. I had a bit of money from my redundancy.
> Everything was happy. I suppose if I didn't have the money, there
> would have been an awful lot of strain. I wouldn't have known how
> to cope, because I've always had a job. I've never been out of work,
> I've always had that bit of money.

Linda felt the strain trying to balance the family budget:

> If the bairns want money for things, we can't get the money. They
> don't understand it. They want to go swimming, and they haven't
> got the money to go swimming, you know, so it's hard to tell them
> that they just can't do it anymore. And clothes, the oldest one, she's
> 11 and she's really growing, and she wants clothes, and we just
> can't afford it. They think it's our fault, that we haven't got money
> for them.
>
> I've never really been one for going out, but if my gran or
> anybody wants to go over to Middlesbrough or anything, I just
> haven't got the money to go with them. I've got to think twice
> about spending any money really. I just haven't got it to spend.

The family budget had been put under even more pressure, because
Linda had had to give up her job, as a part-time cleaner in a local
store.

> I was just doing part-time cleaning, but I've had to pack that in. I
> was having rapid heart beats, and I was told that I was doing too
> much. Stress and overwork, that's what was affecting me, so I've
> been on the sick for four or five weeks, and in the end I've packed
> the job in.
>
> I would consider working again if the right job came along, but I
> would only do part-time. It's usually cleaning or barmaiding – it's
> the only ones that come along. But there's not much for me to do.
> I've not got much chance because I've got no qualifications.
> Sometimes in the paper there's things like going from house to
> house selling fashions. but you need a car.

'Tuppenny halfpenny jobs, aren't they?', chips in Ian. Linda continues:

They're not jobs really. I couldn't go out and do a day's work, because of the children. Unless Ian can't get a job, and he goes back on the dole, then there'd probably be more chance of me getting work than Ian in one of the factories. Round here, there's more jobs for women.

Ian agrees with this: 'You find a lot of these factories round here, they tend to want women. It seems to be that type of job.' The problems with Linda's plan of taking a job is that if Ian does have to go back on the dole, the social security payments that they get towards the mortgage would be hit. Anything that she earned over £4 a week would be knocked off their benefits. 'It's not worth it, financially', he points out. 'Whatever you earn they take off the supplementary benefit.'

Like so many others who had lost their jobs, Ian missed his workmates:

You never see no one. You're stuck in all the time. I mean I'm lucky, because I'm on a training course, so I see a few of the lads, but I never go out. My social life is non-existent. Nil. And the wages I get now, on the bricklaying course are just dole money, that's all it is. I'm actually on supplementary benefit now on top of those wages, just so I can exist.

The loss of Ian's job had also had perceptible effects on family life. 'He seems sometimes withdrawn into himself,' said Linda. 'If I'm upset, I'll show it, but sometimes I think that he doesn't care that he's lost his job, and then he'll come out and say that he does. He keeps it to himself.'

Then I asked Ian for his thoughts on the effects on his home life. They reflected a bewilderment at what had happened to him, a feeling of having little or no control over his own destiny. 'My thoughts? I have no thoughts. What can I do? It's out of my hands. They closed my shipyard down, I've lost my job. That's it.'

As for how they saw their future when Ian finished his course, Linda put it this way:

Probably the way things are now, he'll be back on the dole. There's nothing you can look forward to. Just have to hope we can pull together, and get through it. The way things are we haven't got a future really, not money-wise, but we've got each other, and we've got the bairns, so that's the main thing.

Ian's forecast about what would happen at the end of the bricklaying course turned out to be correct. He did think for a time that there was a possibility that BSEL might 'sponsor' him with a local firm at the end of the course – pay his wages for six weeks while he gained experience, but when I saw him in the summer, he told me:

> I've finished my course, and I've signed on the dole. I've been offered a job at London, but it's piece-work, and I don't think I've got the experience. So I could go to London, and I don't think I'll earn any money. It might end up costing me money.
>
> The impression I've got is that all the work is away, and you've got to travel around with the work, and it's mainly piece-work. I can't compete with the time-served bricklayers. So there's not a lot I can do really. I'm looking for a job on a basic rate, but it's very hard to come by bricklaying.

Life in general had not changed a great deal.

> Money's a big problem, then there's the boredom. What do you do during the day? What do you do when the kids come up to you and say 'Can I have this, can I have that?' What do you say to them? 'I've got no money.' There's nothing else you can say, is there really?'

At Christmas 1987, we interviewed Ian and Linda again. This time we talked to them separately. Linda had gone back to her job, cleaning in a local store, in spite of her poor health, and the fact that social security regulations meant that everything she earned over £4 was knocked off Ian's benefit payments. Linda's boss felt she was a very good worker and was keen to have her back, even though she sometimes had to take time off.

> It gets me out of the house, and they're nice people to work with, but really we're no better off. I'm working for £4, the first £29 is for them, and the other £4 is what I'm working for, but I wanted to come back to work. I mean you can't live in each other's pockets all the time, and it gives us a break from each other. I just enjoy coming out to work and mixing with people because I never used to see anybody at home. And they're all good workmates, they don't just say 'you're the cleaner'. They treat me as one of them, and it's just very nice to be out talking to people.

Linda believes that she is well enough to work, though that is not an opinion shared by Ian.

Ian doesn't like me working. He thinks that I'm not fit enough to come back to work, that I've been poorly, but I keep telling him I'm OK. I was taken poorly last year with my heart. It's not a heart complaint, it's a fast heart rate, and if I do too much work, it sets it going too fast, and that's what's making me ill. For a while I was ill with it, and I'm on tablets now, and I think I stayed off work for about five months. I feel OK at the moment, but there are times when I'm not so well.

I know what I can do, and what I can't do. It's something you learn to live with, and the doctor told me I was my own worst enemy, and not to do too much. But the boss is understanding. I used to carry the mop buckets and the hoovers and everything up the stairs, and now he says to me I must use the lift, not to do too much.

Ian was very unhappy about Linda's going back to work, partly because he was concerned about her health, but partly for other reasons too. 'He thinks that's his responsibility to bring the money in. I think that's silly. You know, in these days, womenfolk go out to work. But as I say I'm not coming out for money. I want to come to work to meet people. I just didn't like sitting at home all day.'

Although Linda's motive for going back to work was not primarily financial, she felt that, looking ahead, there could be sound financial reasons for her sticking at the job. For if Ian were to get a job, then the outlook would change dramatically in their favour. They would get the whole benefit of Linda's pay packet, and there would be two wages coming into the house. Rather than try to get a job when that happened, in Cleveland's bleak economic climate Linda felt it was better to stick with the one she had got, even if, at the moment, the actual rewards were paltry. 'Ian might get a job, and then we will be better off, that's why I keep this job on.'

By now the £8,000 redundancy pay-off had all gone, and the financial realtities of life on the dole were having to be faced. Christmas had produced expense that was hard to cope with.

We haven't got as much as we would normally buy. I've bought a few second-hand things, which I would never do, but it suits what the children want, and because I couldn't afford to buy them new, I've bought them second-hand. We've been going out each week buying little presents, instead of normally we could wait the last couple of weeks and buy on a spending spree. We've done as best we can. I would like to be able to get more, and spend a bit more on each present, but we've managed.

The overall financial scene was bleaker still.

It's been terrible. We've got half the extension done on the house which had to be done, because you've got to have two doors between the kitchen and the toilet, so we had to apply for a second mortgage to cover part of the grant. We could only get a 66 per cent grant, so we had to put money to it. So we got a second mortgage, and that's put us more into debt. But the money, I think we've spent it wisely. We've spent it on the house, with the windows. They all needed replacing, so we've had all new windows. We replaced a lot of the furniture that needed replacing. Everything's gone on the house, we haven't just wasted it.

We find it quite hard now that the redundancy money's gone. We've got to manage on supplementary benefit, and what I'm earning. The children can't do everything they want to do. We've got to put limitations on what they can do, but we still try to put them first. If they need something, they get it before us.

We live from week to week. Some weeks by Tuesday, Wednesday, we've just got no money left. I usually have to go round to my grandmother, and she'll lend us something to see us over until he gets his money. He gets it on a Thursday, and it has to go into the bank and clear first. I get paid on a Friday, then I just give my grandmother the money back, and start again next week.

Linda took a very pessimistic view of Ian's job prospects. The only slim possibility appeared to be to apply to Vickers at Barrow in Furness, on the other side of the country, where they were looking for men to build the Trident submarines.

Ian's got no future – not here on Teesside, and I think he's going to have to go further afield for a job. He's going to apply for a job in Barrow in Furness and hopefully if he gets accepted he'll go away for six months, and then if he likes it, we'd all go there. But Ian said that he doesn't want to go anywhere unless we can go with him, he doesn't want us split up as a family.

If he got the job, then I think they arrange that the family can go and have a look at what the place is like, and then after six months, they would help you to move up to there if you wanted to take it. But there's just nothing here, you've got to accept that now. If he stays here, it's going to be a life on the dole. He's tried everything. He's wrote letters. If he sees jobs in the paper, he's gone looking. He's always at the job centre. There's no one tries as hard as Ian does for a job.

She thinks that the experience of losing his job has changed Ian quite noticeably.

Ian's just not the same. He's withdrawn into himself, very quiet, and he puts a show on when people come. He'll joke about it: 'I don't want a job', and things like that. But you can see that it really does bother him. He just tries to put a brave face on. If people are there, he puts a show on for them. When we're on our own, you can see it's bothering him.

By now Ian had joined the job club run by BSEL. The club provides a couple of rooms where members have access to free telephones, stationery and stamps in order to help them in their search for work. There are typewriters and a photocopier, newspapers – which, it is hoped, carry some suitable job advertisements – and commercial directories in which members can look up names and addresses of companies who are active in fields in which they would like to work. Some members will tell you stories of the telephones being used to ring those *risqué* recorded messages in which models or other glamorous females are supposed to tell all. This may be true, but members are expected to pursue at least 10 job leads a day, and advertisements around the wall of the BSEL Job Club proclaimed that two-thirds of members get jobs. There was also a 'Roll of Honour' which listed the dozen members who had found jobs in the four months since August.

Ian was not totally convinced.

In theory, two-thirds of the people who join the job club get jobs. I don't know how true this is. Up till now, it doesn't seem to be very true. But I thought it was a good thing at first. When I came I had a lot of addresses to write to, and I wrote to all these addresses, and now I seem to have exhausted all the addresses, and I just don't know really what to do now. I find that even labouring jobs, you need certain qualifications which I don't have, so I'm at the end of my tether.

I've wrote about eighty letters, of which a quarter of the firms answer, and the answer is always just the same – you are on file. Nothing, absolutely nothing. I've had one interview. I 'phoned up the personnel manager, and he was adamant that I went down. He insisted. I said wouldn't it be all right just to send a CV, but he said 'No, come down to the factory.' I went to the factory, and approached the foreman on the shop floor, and he said 'Sorry, no jobs.' So I wasted my time.

The jobs that Ian had been looking for were in his old shipyard trade, plating. He still had no hopes of getting a job in the new trade for which his training course was supposed to have equipped him – bricklaying.

I never felt there was any prospect. I've approached firms, and they want time-served. If you mention the skill centre they don't want to know.

A couple of the lads who were on the course with me, they got a job on a building site. They approached the foreman – that's how it works – and bluffed their way in. They said they were time-served, and they started, and at the end of the day, the foreman just went up to the lads and said, 'Look, you're no good. You haven't got the speed. On your way.' There's that many time-served bricklayers on the dole round here, why should they go for skill centre lads?

But did Ian feel he could have done anymore to get a job? 'I don't know. How much does it take? I've wrote a lot of letters. I've 'phoned companies, and – nothing. There's just no jobs. There's nothing.' He was also unhappy about Linda's returning to work.

She doesn't need to go to work. She earns nothing. Whatever she earns, the DHSS takes off me, and my wife's ill. The job makes her ill. I see that at the end of the day when she comes home. Luckily she's got an understanding boss at the moment, who'll give her time off when she's ill. I don't like it, but she says it does her more good than bad. I can't stop her.

Christmas this year, it's been a financial burden obviously. While I was working at Smith's Dock, you saved, it was never really a problem. It's nothing to look forward to when you're worrying about it. The bairns are getting a lot of second-hand gear this year. Normally they would get brand new, but I suppose you've just got to carry on haven't you? So long as the kids are happy.

We didn't used to worry much about debts, but now with all my redundancy money gone, we're just going to have to survive on supplementary benefit, which is going to be difficult obviously, plus they're making it harder in April [this referred to major changes in social security rules being introduced by the government in April 1988], so things are going to be even more difficult.

I don't see no future. Not for me, and I don't see no future for the kids, not in this area. They say things are getting better, but there's nothing happening round here. I've wrote away now for a job in Barrow in Furness. They say there's 10 years' work there. I filled in an application form, but whether anything happens about it, we'll just have to see. It's a big upheaval isn't it, moving?

I think it has changed me. My wife would be able to tell you that. Once I had a future, I've got nothing now. I put on a brave front for my wife, but I just can't see any future.

In February 1988, Ian got a job in Hartlepool, 10 miles from his home. It was no thanks to his bricklaying course. The job was one in which he hoped to be able to use his old plating skills.

I first got the contact from the job centre. The man told me it was a permanent job. He said there was plenty of overtime, could I start on Monday? I went down on the Monday, and when I got there, it wasn't the type of job I'd been doing. I didn't really know what I was doing, and the money wasn't very good at all. Because I was working, I was having to pay for the kids' school meals. I was paying for my own train fares, that was 10 pound a week. In fact, at the end of the day I think I was worse off, and my mates said there was no overtime.

After five weeks, the boss said to me it wasn't working out. I was a luxury he couldn't afford, and he wanted to get rid of me to take on two YTS lads. And at that, I just left.

Ian soon found another job, though. This one used the plating skills he had acquired at Smith's Dock.

This one was through the job centre, and it's turned out OK. While I'm here, it's great. The money's decent, but the gaffer said to me, 'All I can offer you is work when I've got it.' So I don't know when it's going to end.

Life's a bit sweeter now. I have a bit of money, but if this job doesn't turn out, and I end up back on the dole, I'll end up getting penalties. They'll only pay half my mortgage, so I'm frightened really. The dole was safe. Once you learn to live within your means, the money was there every week.

Linda told a similar story.

The first job he got, when he went for the interview, they said it was about £120 a week, and when he actually started the job, it was £110 a week. We were no better than we were on the dole. The job he's got now – he works two half-shifts on a Saturday morning. It's £150 a week take-home pay, so that's good. It gives him something to do. He's not sitting in the house all the time.

In spite of her earlier determination to hang onto her cleaning job, in case Ian found work, Linda had eventually got tired of earning only £4 a week, and given it up. Now Ian was back in work, she was looking for a job again desperately. She too was worried about what might happen if Ian lost his job; not just because of the loss of the mortgage interest payments, but also because of the delay in getting benefits sorted out. 'If he goes back on the dole now, it'll be about three, four, maybe five weeks before it's sorted out, and in that time you get no money. You've got to try and manage, and it's just impossible. You end up borrowing money off everybody.'

For the Dales, though, some good had come out of the experience of redundancy and unemployment.

We got a lot closer. I learned to understand him a lot more, and tried to buck him up when he felt down. When he was on the dole, we shared all the work. He helped round the house, which he never did before, so we got really close that way. Now he's back at work, I miss him a lot. I'm that used to him being there all the time. I could be doing a bit of work, and every couple of hours, we'd stop for a cup of tea. I'm really lonely without him now.

CHAPTER 11

ON A CONTRACT

If everybody's honest, nobody's
got a secure job.
(Wife of former Smith's Dock worker)

Those made redundant at Smith's Dock did gradually find work. In the spring of 1987, only 24 per cent had jobs, but by the summer of 1988, this had risen to 65 per cent. In this chapter, we will be concerned with the kind of jobs they got, and particularly with the number who resorted to 'contract' work – short-term jobs of various degrees of casualness, in stark contrast with the stable working conditions at Smith's Dock.

First, we looked at how people found their jobs. By far the most common explanation – from more than a third – was that they had been told that a job was available by a friend or relative. The next most common source was an advertisement in the paper. Only 10 per cent said they had got work through the job centre; the same number as said they got a job by writing 'on spec' to the firm involved.

Table 36 *How people found their jobs*

	%
Through a friend/relative	36
Newspaper advertisement	14
Job centre	10
Wrote direct to company	10
Through shipyard/BSEL	8
Combination/other (e.g. agency, job club)	24

Some people went into jobs that were dramatically different from those they had done at Smith's Dock. One manual worker got a job as a sales representative that brought with it a company car, another fulfilled a long-held ambition to join the RAF, and another managed a sports centre. When we asked those in work in the autumn of 1987, however, what kind of skills they were using in their new jobs, just over half said they were using the same skills as they had at the shipyard. Only 12 per cent said they had acquired new skills in their new job.

As to which trades were most in demand outside the shipyard, we found that all of the small number of plumbers and electricians in the sample found work in their speciality by the summer of 1988, and out of eight joiners, six had managed to find a job in their old trade. All of the interviewees from the drawing office had found work, though not all at their old trade. Welders and platers had success rates around the average, though some had had to move into new trades to get work, while unskilled ships' cleaners were less successful and labourers significantly less successful.

Among the specialised shipbuilding trades, caulker/burners had a very hard time of it, while shipwrights did surprisingly well, though only two of the nine who had jobs were working at their old trade. On the white collar side, most management grades got jobs, as did a majority of foremen and supervisors, but clerical and secretarial had only a 50 per cent success rate, well below the average of 65 per cent for the whole sample at this time.

Table 37 *Success rate of different trades in finding work*

	No. in sample	No. in work	%
Welders	27	16	59
Platers	20	13	65
Fitters	16	7	44
Labourers	16	6	38
Foremen/supervisors	14	8	57
Shipwrights	12	9	75
Clerical/secretarial	10	5	50
Management	10	7	70
Caulker/burners	10	3	30
Transport/crane drivers	9	4	45
Joiners	8	7	88
Canteen staff	8	4	50
Ships' cleaners	6	3	50
Drawing office	6	6	100
Riggers	5	3	60
Electricians/plumbers	4	4	100

Next we looked at the kind of pay rates that people were enjoying in their new jobs, compared with what they had got at Smith's Dock. As we saw in chapter 4, some economists have taken the view that one of the reasons for high unemployment is that wages have been too high, that people have 'priced themselves out of a job'. The remedy they propose is that if people will accept lower wages, 'price themselves into a job', then unemployment will be reduced. Others argue that it works the other way round, that it is not a case of low wages producing employment, rather that *unemployment* produces low wages, as the higher the unemployment rate goes, the weaker the position of workers, and the stronger the position of employers in the labour market.

So what effect did the high unemployment rate on Teesside have on the pay rates of those Smith's Dock workers who were able to find jobs? At regular intervals, we asked those who were in work how the pay in their new job compared with what they were earning at Smith's Dock. It is worth making the point that, with wage inflation running at around 7 per cent or more, you would expect pay in the new job to be better, on average, than the pay at Smith's Dock, particularly as pay rates at Smith's Dock do not appear to have been excessive (see chapter 3, table 3).

In fact, there were always more people who said the pay in their new job was better than at Smith's Dock, but the margin was never very wide, and, as time passed, the percentage who were getting better pay actually fell slightly. (This suggests that even though there might be more jobs around, pay rates were, if anything, becoming less attractive.) The proportion who were getting less money in their new job tended to stay at around 40 per cent. In addition, in the spring of 1988, we asked the interviewees whether they felt the pay in their new job was 'fair'. Forty-four per cent said they did not.

Table 38 *Pay rate in new job compared with Smith's Dock*

	Better (%)	Same (%)	Worse (%)
Round 2	50	9	41
Round 4	50	16	34
Round 7	42	18	40
Round 8	45	14	41

We also asked people to compare their new job with their old job at the yard using criteria other than pay. The areas in which the new jobs scored considerably better than Smith's Dock were safety and job satisfaction. (It is interesting to note, however, that, in the diaries that we asked members of our sample to complete (see chapter 6), those who were in work tended to simply enter 'work'. Very few said anything about what they did at work. There was no account of high points or low points. People were much more descriptive about their leisure time. This might suggest that job satisfaction was not generally high.)

We have already seen that companionship was considered to be one of the major benefits of working at Smith's Dock, and, in this respect, the new jobs just did not compare. Nearly 40 per cent said companionship was worse than at Smith's Dock, more than three times the number who said it was better.

Perhaps the most important areas, though, in which the new jobs were felt to be inferior were fringe benefits and security of employment. In every case, they came out substantially worse than at Smith's Dock, pointing strongly to a movement towards casualisation.

Table 39 *How new job compares with job at Smith's Dock*

	Better (%)	Worse (%)
Companionship	12	39
Job security	26	50
Safety	40	23
Wages/pay	45	41
Hours of work	27	33
Job satisfaction	36	20
Holidays	15	43
Pensions/fringe benefits	22	47

Although the difference between those who said hours of work were worse in their new job and those who said they were better is fairly narrow, it is clear that in their new jobs, many people did work extremely long hours. More than a fifth of those in work did a basic week of more than 40 hours, with 5 per cent working more than 45 hours, including one man who claimed to be working up to 70 hours a week, and one up to 84 hours.

In addition, some worked substantial amounts of overtime. More than half said they worked six hours or more, and 18 per cent worked 13 hours or more. The diaries compiled by those in work revealed that 20 per cent worked six days a week, and 12 per cent worked seven days a week.

Job security was seen as a key issue by most people we interviewed. Eight-six per cent said they agreed with the statement that 'A job with security is more attractive than a job with a high level of pay.' In the summer of 1987, though, 40 per cent of those in work said they felt insecure in their jobs, and about the same proportion were applying for other jobs.

In keeping with this, the research demonstrated that there was a constant movement in and out of work. So, between the spring and summer of 1987, for example, 30 people had found jobs, but 12 people had lost jobs. Fourteen people found work in the autumn of 1987, only to lose their jobs by Christmas. In each case, 10 of the interviewees said they had been in temporary jobs. In addition, it is worth noting that 12 per cent of the jobs found by the spring of 1988 were part-time; two-thirds of these being held by women. By then, only 16 per cent of the sample had not had a job at all since leaving the yard, but only a half were at that time in work.

Throughout the survey, a large proportion of those in work said they were in temporary or contract jobs. In the summer of 1987, the figure was 46 per cent. In the spring of 1988, the figure was 40 per cent, while by the summer, it had reached almost a half. Of those who described themselves at this point as working in temporary jobs, only a third were on a formal contract. The rest had a more casual arrangement.

We used other measures too to quantify this casualisation of the labour market. At the end of 1987, for example, we questioned people who had had other jobs since leaving the yard, but then left them, about why they had gone. The main answer, from almost half, was that their contract had come to an end.

In the winter of 1987, we asked people how many jobs they had had since leaving the yard. A hundred people answered. Of those who had worked since Smith's Dock closed, more than a third had done more than one job, and scores of three or more were not unusual. Indeed, there were some who claimed to have done as many as eight jobs.

Table 40 *Number of jobs held by interviewees since Smith's Dock closed*

No. of jobs	Currently employed	Currently unemployed
1	43 people	16 people
2	12 people	10 people
3	4 people	2 people
4	4 people	3 people
6	0	3 people
8	0	3 people

At various points in the study we looked at the particular problem of contract work. In the autumn of 1987, a quarter of those on contracts told us they were employed for less than three months, while a half said they did not know how long their contracts were for. At the time, 26 per cent said they disliked contract working.

In the summer of 1988, there were complaints from 6 per cent of those on contracts that they could not get credit, while a further 16 per cent said they were worried about the job ending, and their not being able to get another. Others said that no one dared complain about anything in case they got the sack. One reported overhearing a foreman say, 'Anyone who complains about safety round here will get his cards.' Sixty-one per cent, though, said that contract work did not cause any particular problems. When, however, we asked those working on contracts what they saw as the advantage of this arrangement, 68 per cent said it had no advantages.

Case study

In the winter of 1987, a 'For Sale' sign stood outside the semi-detached house in Billingham owned by Dave and Alison Waller. It had stood there for a few months, and would stand for a few months longer. Houses in Billingham do not move quickly, even when they are on pleasant new estates like this one.

Dave had been a night shift welder at Smith's Dock for five years. His father and brother had both worked there. He and Alison had known each other since they were nine. Their parents lived 10 doors apart. Dave had left the yard early, in August 1986, in order to get on a pipe-welding course, which he thought would improve his skills and give him a better chance of a job. Three months later, the couple's first child, Sarah, was born.

Dave was partly right about the course's giving him a better chance of finding a job. The first job he got was at a factory where his father-in-law was a manager. The problem was that he did not get it until May 1987, by which time most of his redundancy money had run out. As with most of the jobs available for welders, this one was on a short-term contract, lasting for three months.

Dave's luck was still in, though, because two days after leaving that job, he landed another temporary contract at Sunderland Ship-builders.

I got a job at a pipework firm. That was a three-month contract. Two days after I was laid off, I got a letter from BSEL saying there was a temporary job going up at Sunderland, and I took that job. It was meant to run for just two or three weeks, and it lasted 12 weeks. After that I've been on the dole ever since.

At this point the Wallers found themselves trapped by the change in supplementary benefit rules introduced in 1987, which limited the payment of mortgage interest. It meant the Wallers would be about £85 a month worse off. In addition to that, because they had an endowment mortgage, they had to pay £25 a month on a life insurance policy, for which they received no assistance.

'It's affected us quite badly', said Alison.

We got less money than we did last time he was on the dole, because by the time we've paid all our bills out, we only have 20 pound a week to buy food and things for Sarah, and everything. So we can't manage, and if it wasn't for our parents, we wouldn't be able to live properly. We buy what we can out of our 20 pound, but we normally have to go to our parents and borrow something until we get the next lot of dole, but then you're like in a chain aren't you? You have to pay back what you owe before you can start again, so it doesn't really help.

I feel guilty about borrowing money off our parents, because they're working for their money, and they're earning their money, so they shouldn't have to keep us as well. They do help us a great deal and we do appreciate it, but it's just the fact that we should be getting enough money to support us off the social security, and it's annoying to know that you're not.

Dave was forthright about how he felt about having to borrow from their parents:

Rotten, in a word. Hopefully, I can pay them back for what they've done one day, if I get a job, or if I sell the house. I don't think it's right that some days they come up with bags of shopping or something like that, and say 'We've bought you some food', and you just feel like beggars. It's not nice at all.

For the Wallers, as for most of the families affected by the closure of Smith's Dock, Christmas 1987 was not a lot of fun. This was how Alison saw it:

Last Christmas we had David's redundancy, so we managed well last year. This year we've had to struggle to get Sarah's things, and things for the family. They've been understanding, and they've said, 'Don't bother about us', but you still feel as though you should get them something. And we haven't done anything about getting food for Christmas coming. It's been a struggle. We're not going to be able to go out as much as we wanted to, but we'll just have to manage.

Dave saw the prospects similarly: 'Christmas is a time of going out, enjoying yourself, buying presents, but this year we can't do any of that really. There's no money coming in, so we're not going to get anything unless my parents and Alison's parents can let us have some. They've been very helpful.'

The Wallers were doing what they could to reduce their need to borrow from the family. Dave's pride and joy was an 'N' registration Rover car, which he had had done up and kept in good condition, and which was worth around £1,000.

I'm selling the car to try and get money for Christmas, or to pay off some debts. Hopefully it'll sell before Christmas but, if not, I'll just have to wait. I want money for Christmas so we can enjoy it and buy presents and things, because I feel we should do after the help we've got off our parents.

It's sad. I've had it for three years. It was a piece of scrap when I got it, and there's been a lot of money spent on it, I've worked hard on it. It's just sad that you've got to sell something that you really love to bring money into the house. I don't think it should come to that. I think the social should give us enough money to live on, and at the moment they're not. We've got to get money to live on. We can't keep living off our parents.

Alison had similar feelings about the decision to sell the car: 'I know how much the car means to David, and I don't really want him to have to sell it, because I don't want him to regret it afterwards, and I don't think he should have to sell it. I'm sad as well, because I've got attached to it, but we're going to have to do it.'

The house, which they had lived in for less than two years, had also been put up for sale. This decision was more complicated. Alison was pregnant, and when their second child was born, it would be too small, though they recognised that if they sold this house, they would not be able to buy another until Dave had got a job.

We put the house up for sale about three months ago, because I'm expecting another baby, and we need another bedroom. We haven't had much interest, but we're hoping it will pick up after the New Year. Now if we sell the house while David's unemployed, we're going to have to go and live with his parents, which won't be really good for us or for them. It's like intruding on their privacy as well, but we would cope, I think. We'd all have to just help each other until he got employment, and then we could get another mortgage for another property. So we're not really in a rush at the moment, and we'll just have to wait and see what happens.

'I think it would be good if we did sell the house,' added David, 'because from the money we would make on it, we could pay the odd debt or two off. It would be hard to live at my mum's again, but we're just going to have to muck in together, because without a job, to be honest, I can see myself living at my mum's quite a while.'

This was a prediction based on Dave's assessment of his prospects of finding a steady job.

I need a permanent job. There's nothing for me here at the present time. I think maybe in four or five years' time, Teesside will get back on its feet. I think the industry will start to come up again, but at the moment, there's only short-term contracts. They usually last for three months, and I need to be laid off at about eight weeks to make any money out of the job.

Dave was now in a classic catch-22 introduced by the new social security regulations on mortgage payments. Suppose you were unemployed before January 1987, and you had a mortgage. The DHSS met all your interest payments. In spite of the rule change of January 1987, if you remained unemployed, this arrangement continued for you as an existing claimant. Then, suppose you get the chance of a temporary job lasting, say, three months. Being conscientious, enterprising, keen on work, and all those other things the Government is supposed to like, you take it. At the end of it, you cannot find another job. Now, though, because you are a new claimant, you are affected by the new regulations. So for the first four months of unemployment, you lose half your mortgage interest payments. Your penalty for having taken a job is, in the case of the Wallers, about £350.

There is a way round this. If you take a job that lasts eight weeks or less, it does not count as having interrupted your period of unemployment. So you stay on full mortgage interest payments. All right, then, why not just walk off the job after eight weeks, however

long the contract may be? This is where the catch-22 comes in. If you
do that, you could be considered to be intentionally unemployed, and
you might have *all* your benefit suspended. The upshot of this maze of
regulations is that people in Dave's position have to think very
carefully before they take a job. Will the pay they get be enough to
offset the loss of mortgage payments?

Not surprisingly, Dave had been thinking about this. 'It's not
worth me taking a short-term job. The arears on the mortgage are
about £300 now, and I'll have to find that out of the wages from the
next job I do get, and I'll just be starting all over again. It's not worth
me working.'

Alison's views were similar.

There's nothing really in David's line of work that's going to be
permanent. It's all going to be just short-term, and it's going to be a
case of in and out of work all the time, and you're in a chain. You're
going back onto half mortgage for four months, and it's just never
going to end. After I've had this baby, I would go back to work if it
came to that. There's probably more for me to do than there is for
David's side, but that would be a last resort. I wouldn't want to do
that really because it would mean David staying at home with the
children and everything.

David's reservations about this idea was based on his belief that it
was the man's responsibility to fulfil the role of breadwinner.

I don't think it would be right for a start-off. It's down to me to
bring some sort of money in. I think I'll be all right with the
children. I'll manage that side of it all right. It's just I wouldn't like
Alison to go out to work and me being sat at home looking after the
children, when I should be out at work, and bringing in the money.

CHAPTER 12

GOING IT ALONE

I'm going to try and go it alone.
There's nothing else for me.
(Steve Gatley)

One of the vogue words of Mrs Thatcher's Government has been 'enterprise'. It set up an Enterprise Allowance scheme for those unemployed people prepared to set up their own business. There was talk of re-naming the Department of Trade and Industry as the Department of Enterprise. Above all, there was promulgation of the 'enterprise culture'. This was going to replace what was rather condescendingly referred to as the 'dependency culture', which was supposed to have grown up in areas of high unemployment like Teesside.

In the view of the crudest advocates of 'enterprise', this meant the unemployed should stop whingeing, get up off their backsides, and start their own business. It went a bit further than that, though. The idea was based on a belief that the small businesses of today were where the jobs of tomorrow would come from, as they grew into ever bigger businesses, helping to regenerate the local economy. That from the ashes of the smokestacks, or in this case the shipyard, might arise the pheonix of enterprise. This all had a fair head of political steam behind it, and it did make some impact. No less than 41 per cent of our sample told us they had considered setting up their own business.

Getting a business off the ground, though, is seldom as simple as it looks. In an area as depressed as Teesside was at the time of Smith's Dock's closure, the obstacles are formidable indeed, the most obvious being that with so many people out of work, money was short and potential customers had little to spend on the products of a business. By the end of 1987, our sample provided only seven entrants to the 'enterprise culture' – less than 4 per cent of those interviewed. During the first half of 1988, another four individuals had followed them, though one of the original seven had gone out of business, leaving ten. Two of the people (a husband and wife) were in the same business – a sub-post office and general dealer. (Ray Snaith, whose story comes at the end of this chapter, was not part of our sample.) Of the other businesses, two involved fishermen, and the rest – a milkman, a groundsman, a joiner, a welder, a heating and plumbing engineer and a seller of artwork. In spite of the Government's promises of encouragement, help and advice to those wanting to go it alone, only three of the ten had gone to an official agency, and four had taken no advice at all.

Only two had gone on the Enterprise Allowance Scheme. Nor did BSEL feature heavily in their plans. Although one of its jobs was to help Smith's Dock workers who wanted to set up their own businesses, only one of the ten had taken a loan from it. Caution seemed the order of the day, in that six of the ten had not taken out any loans at all to start their business. Most seemed reasonably happy with their decision to go self-employed, and certainly no one said they would have preferred to be on the dole. None the less, it is hard to see these enterprises as great generators of the jobs of tomorrow. We can be sure that they are not great generators of jobs today. Only three of the businesses had any other employees: one employed two people, and the other two one each.

So what degree of commitment did our small number of self-employed people have to the 'enterprise culture'? Revealingly, six of the ten said they would give up their business if they were offered a job.

Still, scepticism as to whether the 'enterprise culture' can solve Teesside's employment problem does not prevent admiration for those individuals who tried to make a go of it in an area where the difficulties were so daunting. They are a small group of people, but the stories are so vivid that I have included two.

Case study 1

On the opposite bank of the River Tees from central Middlesbrough is Port Clarence, where the population is sufficiently small and close-knit to be appropriately described by that overworked word 'community'. There are some rows of old terraced council houses in streets named after public schools. (It would be interesting to know who was the last inhabitant to go to Eton or Harrow.) In one of these, Steve Gatley lived with his common law wife Christine and their four children.

Steve, then a plater aged 24, lost his job at Smith's Dock in October 1986. Like most of those made redundant, Steve was upset by the closure: 'I don't think it should have been closed. It was the best yard in the north-east of England.' Nor did he have any illusions about how tough the labour market would be.

At the most I would say 25 per cent will get jobs, especially in the North-east. There's nothing at all for us. There's about 2,000 – 3,000 lads going for one job. There's nowhere in Cleveland. You've got to go way out, abroad, and most lads who are married with families, their wives won't let them do it.

Unlike most of those made redundant, though, Steve was not bewildered at finding himself out of a job, and he had a very clear idea of where he was going.

I've put in for a fish and chip shop, and I'm going to try and go it alone. There's nothing else for me. I'm scared to go on the dole, I don't want to go on the dole at all. So I'm going to make a go of it. I hope it succeeds. I hope to be a successful businessman and start up young people. I hope to start my own brother up when he leaves school.

Steve received a redundancy pay off of £5,500 with which to try to further his ambition. The shop that he had chosen was in a rather rundown parade a short distance from his home. Once it had been run by his mother and father, but they had given it up. Then it had operated as a Chinese takeaway, before closing down.

By April of 1987, Steve had been on the dole he was so afraid of for six months, but at least he was now tantalisingly close to achieving his ambition.

I've been on a fish-frying course at Cleethorpes. I learned about VAT, and how to fry fish and chips, and where to buy them from. I've had advice from a Community Employment Development Officer. He comes and helps unemployed people start up in their own business.

I've also done market research. I made some questionnaires out for people in the local area, and also people who use the pubs and clubs with different questions for different people. And there's all the works around here. One's just won a big order, and they're getting more workers in, and I felt that was beneficial for me. So I went out with some market research, and I asked them to fill these forms in. Questions like: would you eat fish and chips if there was a fish and chip shop here? Would you use it at all, and if it was open and there was a free delivery service, would you 'phone in?

And, of course, most of them said 'yes', and I got them all to sign the research sheets to make sure that it was true, and I produced them to the CEDO officer [Community Employment Development Officer]. I think it was 97/98 per cent of them said they would use a fish and chip shop, which is very satisfactory. Another question was, where do you get them from now? Most people have said Billingham and Stockton, and the closest one to where my fish and chip shop is now is three miles away, and people have to get buses, or get cars out, and it's very inconvenient for them, and it's cost them a lot because they're paying for their petrol or their bus fare. So I'll benefit from all these people.

I found all this out, and I made my business plan. I approached BSEL for a business loan – it's very low interest, see. They interviewed me. There was a bank manager, a director and what have you. They had a look, and they sent me a letter saying 'you can have the loan, no problem'. They're very satisfied with my business plan, it was that good. See I've worked on it since October, and it's April now, and I've gone through it thoroughly. I've had electricians in, I've had plumbers in, I've had fitters in, estimating how much it'll cost me to do the shop out. See, I paid for that, and the BSEL money, that'll be paying for the machinery.

For someone whose whole experience of work had been confined to the shipyard, Steve adapted remarkably quickly and comfortably to the alien world of the 'enterprise culture'.

I'm just in the process of signing my lease, which I've had a few arguments over in the past few months. We've had it changed two or three times, my solicitor and I. Now we're happy with it, and we've agreed to it, and I'm just waiting for a call from my solicitor to tell me to come up and sign it.

Starting up a business, I never thought it was so difficult. You've got to get a solicitor, an accountant, you've got to get your insurance brokers. Also opening a fish and chip shop business, you've also got to get environmental health, you've got to get pest control. You've got to sort out what you're going to do inside the shop, outside the shop. It's very hard, but enjoyable.

At the moment, I'm stripping all the old boards off, and I was going to tile it, but I'm not now, I'm going to wallpaper it. Also the kitchen, I'm going to wallpaper that. I'm going to do all the floors and strip the range completely down, clean it up and put it back together again. My brother's father-in-law, who's a time-served painter and decorator, he's going to do all the painting and decorating with me.

When I refurbish it, I want it to look good. Everything in there's got to be good quality. The more customers there are in there, the happier I'll be. I'm putting in a suggestion box. If people don't like anything, they can come and tell me. I've thought of everything for the shop. It took me a long time, because I want the fish shop to be a success for me and the family as well.

Plus, round here there's a lot of unemployment, and I'm starting up local people, like my brother. He's leaving school, and I'm going to start him up, and I'm going to teach him the trade, and send him on a course of what I've been on. So eventually I'm going to own more than one and I'd like my brother to run one of the fish shops for me. I'd like to buy one at the seaside eventually, but at the moment I've got to concentrate on one, and make sure it's a success.

I've got a few ambitions. I want my family on a lovely holiday abroad. I've never been abroad. None of the family ever have. I want to take my mam and dad abroad. My dad, being in the navy, he's been abroad, but my mother never has, and she'd love to go, and I'd love to pay for it for her. And my other ambition is to own a Rolls Royce. Not a new one, but a Rolls Royce. That's my ambitions.

Steve saw his involvement in setting up the fish shop as having saved him from some of the worst of the psychological effects of unemployment being suffered by his former workmates. It was a view based on his own experiences during the months before he had got the project going. 'It was terrible at first. All I was doing was drinking in the local pubs and clubs, and I realised it was no good. I had to do something, because my money was just going to waste, and I was making a terrible life for myself.'

It's been hard for Christine more than me, like when I was going out, I used to come in drunk, which I did quite often until I started on the fish shop, and it was terrible. I used to come in, have a meal, go to bed, get up and go out again. It's not a life, honestly. I had to pull my socks up. That's when I started with my CEDO officer. I approached a solicitor and the council about the fish and chip shop, and then we started working on it, and since then, it's been all go. It's been fantastic. I get on better with Christine and the children. I take them out often, so it's no trouble now.

If I hadn't got the fish shop, honestly I'd have had no redundancy left. I'd be one of the lads on the dole. I'd be on that all the time, and that's not me. I know for a fact that if I didn't have this fish shop, I'd be a plonky [drunkard]. I know it's a terrible thing to say, but that's all I would do. That's no life.

Steve had suffered from the closure in other ways.

The main thing is I don't see many people now. I miss the relationships with my workmates. Round the house, it's funny, I change nappies, I wash up, do this, do that, hoover up. I've even done a bit of gardening, and it's not me that. But it's friendship I've missed.

The family budget had also been affected. 'Things we'd like to do we can't,' said Steve. 'We were going to go on holiday, but I said, "No, we need the money for the shop," which I do. But I said, "In a few years' time, we'll have one abroad, and I can't wait for it." You see in the long run, it'll work out.'

Christine took a similar view about the adverse effect that the closure of the yard had had on Steve, and about how the fish shop had mitigated it.

It was hard for him, being in the house all the time, going out drinking. He had nothing to do. He was very bored, which is natural. That's why he's been doing things round the house, keeps his mind occupied. It was a strain at first, being on top of each other all the time. He's been going to the club, like to pass the time away, because it is long days when there's nowt to do, where he's been used to a job all the time, hasn't he, working?

But now it's different. With him knowing he's got the fish and chip shop, he's been doing a lot of work, I don't really see him much, so we get on better now. I'm over the moon. He's got something to look forward to. I know it's going to be hard at first for him, but everything will work out, won't it?

Christine had suggested that she might help out in the shop, but Steve was against it.

Christine, she's argued with me over it. She wants to work in the fish shop, and I'm not going to let her. I don't want her under my feet at work. The children want to know at least one parent, and, with me, I'll be up before them to prepare everything at the fish shop, and I'll be in late, and they'll be in bed, and I'd sooner them know their mother and their father, but they can't know them both, with me in business. They've got no chance of seeing me, so they may as well see their mother. I know it's going to be a sin on the kids, and also on me for not seeing them. Only time I'll see them is when they're in bed asleep, and I can't exactly wake kids up in the night, can I, wake them up saying, 'Dad's here'? It's no good, but I will have one day a week off, and I'll be taking them out. I'll be looking forward to it – it'll be a break from the shop, but I'm looking forward to starting up as well.

After their discussion, Christine had come around to a similar view.

Sitting with Steve the other night, I said I'd like to help out a couple of hours a week, but I said working all the time in there, we'd be under each other's feet. And he doesn't like anyone arguing with him, nor do I like anybody telling me what to do. So it wouldn't work out between us in the fish shop.

For Steve, the closure of Smith's Dock now appeared to have been a blessing in disguise. It had forced him to explore new avenues, to find abilities within himself that perhaps he never realised were there.

People who have got jobs, they never think of starting up their own business until redundancy sets in, and then that's the time to think. You have no choice, you've got to. Now, in a way, I'm glad I got made redundant. I'm starting up my own business, and for me, that's the only good thing that Maggie Thatcher's ever done for the North-east. Just from my point of view, nobody else's, but I'll still be voting Labour.

Steve also recognises, though, that the number of redundant shipyard workers who feel inclined to enter the 'enterprise culture' may be fairly small.

I've approached two lads that live in the next street, and they got paid off, made redundant the same time as me, and they got a lot more redundancy money than me, because they're older. And I've asked them if they're going to do anything, and they're not. They're quite content going out, having a few pints, and going home. Honestly, I couldn't do that. I tried it at first, but it's no good. For me, it's just a waste of time. I'm sick of trying to tell them, but they won't have it, it's their lives. They run it how they like.

Most people say, 'We've had our whack. We're not going to get a job. We'll enjoy spending our money.' Now when that's gone, they'll be down in the dumps. It'll be terrible for them, they won't have anything to do, apart from join that long dole queue.

Two months later, Steve was in business. The shop was open. He had been enterprising enough to get the local Labour MP, Frank Cook, to do the official opening. The local paper headlines trilled out the story of the lad sacked from Smith's Dock, who was starting to make good: 'Steve batters the dole blues', 'Steve's recipe for success', and so on.

He had to invest his redundancy money, and borrow £5,500 – £4,000 from BSEL, and another £1,500 from the bank. In addition, he had received a £750 grant from BSEL, and he had gone on the Government's Enterprise Allowance scheme. Not surprisingly, Steve was delighted that he had finally got the shop open, eight months after losing his job at the yard.

I'm glad I've got a job. It's long hours, but I don't mind putting them in. I work nearly 14 hours a day in here, and I do all my books. That's as well as all the preparation. I was sick the first week for working such long hours, but now I'm enjoying it. I know how to do it, see? I get home earlier now.

It's been going very well. I predicted so many sales for so many people, and I'm getting a lot more in. I'm getting a lot more orders from the local industries now. I have a lot of tanker drivers stopping off as well. Plus I'm waiting for a 'phone to get in to get my 'phone-in orders. I've had a lot of workmen asking for that. I'm very confident. I won't leave this place now. I'm looking forward to buying another one.

Buoying up Steve's hopes was the knowledge that the local council was investing in the refurbishment of the rather down-at-heel parade of shops in which his fish shop was sited.

The way I look at it is that it can't get any worse. It must get better. They've got the money for the buildings. I'm getting a new shop front in here shortly, I'm getting central heating, a new fitted kitchen, and a new fitted bathroom. Plus I've been to see the council about all the area, and so I'm getting re-modernised, re-furbished.

For the moment, though, he had to take a long-term view of the business. He could foresee a time when it would be a real money-spinner, but that time was not yet.

I was earning more at the dock, believe it or not. For three weeks now, I haven't paid myself a penny. I have that many overheads, I can't afford to pay myself yet, and people think I'm earning a fortune. I'm not, not yet. But in the future, four or five years' time, I'll be on my feet.

So how long would it take until he was equalling his earnings from Smith's Dock?

A couple of months. That's my forecast. It's very promising. I've got myself established in here. It's looking great. You see when I pay off my loan from BSEL, and I start making money, I'll be putting it away for the future, for my sons and daughters, and also the woman in my life. In the future, I hope to start my children up myself, and give them a shop of their own. It was hard for me, but it won't be hard for my children. It won't be as hard as I had it. They'll have a better chance.

Steve's confident view about his own future, though, was in striking contrast to his foreboding about the future of his former workmates, and of Teesside generally.

All shipyard trades now are dying trades. You've got no chance of getting a job now. It's six weeks here, six weeks there. I can't see a future on Teesside. I can't see many jobs being made in the North-east now. If they want a job now, they've got to work in the South, unless they want to start their own business.
  You've got to have get-up-and-go, and most people round here are so sick of people promising them so many things and they've never had it. So nobody's bothered. But the likes of me. I've

worked since I was 16. I'm 25 now, and I was scared of going on the dole. I couldn't live on the dole.

Like I said earlier, Margaret Thatcher in some respects, she's done good for me, and Labour's done good for me. They were giving one-parent families and the unemployed a lot more money than Mrs Thatcher is. She was looking after the people with the money. The downfall is that the one-parent family and the unemployed won't get as much, so they can't spend as much in the shop, which I'd like them to. So it's merely the people that work that come in and spend the money. It's not the people who are unemployed. They come in maybe once or twice a week when they get paid, but that's all.

Since the shop opened, Christine had seen a new Steve.

He's a different person altogether. He's more active. He's happy when the customers come in the shop. I mean everybody likes him. He doesn't go out much now, so that's quietened him down to what he used to be. And the shop keeps him going. He's not in the way all the time now.

He goes in and unlocks the shop at nine o'clock in the morning. He does all his fish, and I go down when I take the kids to school. You walk in, and he's whistling with his dad. One time he used to be moping round the house, or going out drinking. Now we just get on better because we talk to each other. He tells me his problems, what happens in the shop. If anything gets on top of him, he'll talk to me about it, and I'll talk to him.

In spite of their earlier decision that Christine would not work in the shop, she did.

He said 'You're not working, because I don't believe in a woman working.' Then when it opened, he said, 'I'd like you to come in.' Now he likes me working there, he says to me I'm a big help. I don't like being stuck in the house on my own all the time. By the time you've done your work and you've got your kids to bed, there's nothing to do for yourself, and going down to work's great. It's very hard work, you're busy all the time, but the laughs you get! Sometimes he thinks I'm an octopus, you know what I mean. 'Get this, get that', while he's stood there doing his frying. But me, I'd work all the time, I would.

Like Steve, she now saw the closure of the shipyard as having been a blessing in disguise.

When he was at Smith's Dock, he was on about packing it in, and going to work away, and I was a bit upset over that. But then he was changing his mind all the time, and when they finally got made redundant, he set his heart on this fish shop and got it. If he was still at Smith's, he'd be moody all the time. I mean he's got something for the future now when he didn't then really.

He said like a few years' time, we'll have money. I mean it takes years to build up a business, doesn't it? And he said we'll have a future to live. We're going to travel places. He wants to do more fish shops, but he said we'll be comfortable, we'll have a lovely home then, and we'll want for nothing, and that's what we're really looking forward to. I'd like to go on working. I said to Stephen I'd like to do a business myself. When it's getting near Christmas I'd like to go to a warehouse, get toys in, and do a toy party in the house, so that I can do a business myself.

By December 1987, though, Steve and Christine had received an object lesson in just how difficult it is to get a business off the ground in a depressed area. They had been moved out to Billingham. Their old house had been boarded up, as had three whole streets around the fish and chip shop, as part of a major development scheme. The effect on Steve's market had been dramatic.

The council was selling three streets off where the shop was. A gentleman from the council was coming showing people houses, and asking them where they'd like to go to and when. Then when they decided they wanted to move, they'd start boarding all the houses up. Gradually this was going on week by week, and the tenants around the area were getting less and less. With everybody moving out, an average of four or five in a family, it's a heck of a lot of trade for me to lose. And, of course, I had to shut nights because there was nobody there to sell food to. And also one of the factories they've been paying off, and they're not guaranteed a new order till the New Year, and that means all I had tradewise was a few people that were left, and also the passing trade of the tankers. If it wasn't for them, I'd have had to shut earlier on.

When I first opened up, there was my mother, my father, Chris and I, we were all working there full time, six afternoons, six nights. It was going fantastic. I was ordering double everything. Fish, chips, everything. And as people were moving out, I was ordering less and less. Then when I had to shut nights, one of my staff had to go, because I couldn't afford them. That meant my mother and I had to work more because I had to finish my father. See my father can't serve or fry, he was just the lad in the back. It's one of the worst things I've ever done in my life, finish my father with him being family. I approached him and I told him what was going on, and he said he's sorry about the business not working out, and I couldn't do anything about it. He offered to stay on for no money at all, but I just couldn't let it happen. It's one of the sorriest things I've ever had to do in my life. I could never do it again.

I kept my mother on and myself, and with us not being so busy I also didn't want Chris to come in part-time neither. Me and my mother were just running it by ourselves. At some stages, one of us could run it, not two, just one frying and serving. That's how bad it was getting.

As the three streets finally went, I just couldn't afford to pay my bills. My BSEL loan, that's £385 a quarter. Then I had my personal loan to pay. Also I had my till to pay for, the staff to pay for, gas and electric to pay for. It was just too much. I couldn't afford the overheads. I was making on what I was selling, but it wasn't making enough, so I couldn't afford to pay all the bills, and that's why I've had to close down.

I'm trying to get a buyer for the shop. It'll go for next to nothing because of the area. There's no one living down there, and plus all the industries have laid people off. With it closing down, I owe £4,000 to BSEL, which I don't know how I'm going to pay back. I'm worried sick over that. My personal loan out to the bank, I can meet the requirements of the monthly repayments, that's not too much trouble, but also I've lost all my redundancy pay which I put into it, and that is totally disheartening to me.

From Christine's point of view, the decline and closure of the shop had been an equally traumatic experience.

When he opened the shop, it was all go, it was great, everybody was coming in. Then they started emptying the three terraces out and as things started to go down in the business, Steve was getting worried, everything was getting on top of him, and then we ended up fighting. I've been worried because I know Stephen doesn't like the dole. He likes to be working, he likes to be doing something all the time.

Now he's having to sell the business, I do feel sorry for him, because he put a lot into it, he did, a lot of hard work, all of his money, and it's just a bad letdown for him. I mean the surveys he went round with, people saying they'd come in the shop, you didn't see hardly any of them. It was just passers-by, lorry drivers. He's been very moody. It's a horrible thing for him. He's put everything into it, and this is what's happened. He was thinking of our future, the children's, and nothing really worked out. There's nothing we can do about it now really. He's just had to give it all up. I'm just hoping something turns up better for him.

The collapse of the business meant that Steve and Christine were suddenly faced with the dilemma of how they were going to pay for Christmas. Steve solved it by taking out a further loan of £1,000, which meant that he was now more than £6,000 in debt.

We were frightened because we didn't have any money to get the kids' stuff. Anyway, then Steve went for a bank loan, and we went out last week to get the majority of the kids' toys in. We still have a few more to buy, but if it wasn't for Stephen, we wouldn't have had anything.

Everything's turned out better than we thought it would have, because all we were was a bag of nerves with the worry of the kids and everything.

Christine was concerned, though, about their having had to take on more debt in order to pay for Christmas.

It's money to pay back. It's still a debt, but we're not really worried about that at the moment as long as we see the kids with a good Christmas. That's all we wanted.

Last Christmas we managed smashing. Stephen was just out of work then, we had his redundancy. The Christmas before we managed smashing. We had the money there, and we could go out and get what we wanted. It's just this year we've had a struggle, with Steve in the shop and everything.

Steve too felt that going for the loan had been the correct course of action. 'We've spent most of the money now. We've got a few more gifts to get, but that'll be enough. We might have to stay in quite a few nights over Christmas. We won't be able to afford to go out, but at least we've got the children their clothes, plus the toys they need.'

In spite of the failure of the shop that had hit him so hard, and left him with such formidable financial problems, Steve was still glad he had a go at starting a business.

I'm glad I did. See, I've done everything right. I've done my market research. I went house to house, I went to pubs, I went to clubs. I even went to works. I put posters up. I approached BSEL. It must have been good market research, because they allowed me the loan. It was in good premises. I did it all myself, and it was due to get modernised as well. But, no, I don't regret it one bit.

I would definitely go in business again. It's hard, you put a lot of hours in. It's very committing, but if the right opportunity came along, I would definitely do it again. See, with me, I don't like the dole. I never have done. I never will do. It's just that I'm a working lad. I love work, and that's it. I'll try to get a job, and I'll save the money, but I'll definitely go in business. In what I don't know, but I'll do it.

Christine, though, showed a marked reluctance to contemplate any more forays into the 'enterprise culture'.

Oh, I don't know if I could stand it. It's nerve-racking being in your own business. It's a lot of strain, pressure, it's an awful lot of pressure. And the only person Steve could really talk to, and, like, shout at if anything was bothering him was me. I could understand him sometimes, but it was very hard on me as well, and it is a lot of responsibility, and I don't think I could go through it again. It's not like just getting a job. It's worry, it's all worry.

The only immediate future she could see was one in which she and Steve would be apart.

What future is there? There's no jobs round here, and we're going to be apart from each other. He's got to go away to work, which I don't want, but it's where the money is. We would see him every weekend or whatever. It depends how long he's away for, but it might be a better future for us.

Steve's view was the same.

It's bleak at the moment. I've got to find a job. Like Christine was saying, I'll have to go away to work. She doesn't want me to, but

I'll go. It's where the money is, it's the way I can save. I've worked away before, so I know I can do it. It's for the family. It's not just for me. We have four young children. We've got to have a brighter future for them, not just us.

Case study 2

New Marske is not much more than a modern housing estate a few miles east of Middlesbrough, close to the sea. For a year, a decaying fish and chip van cluttered up one of the suburban drives outside its neat semi-detached houses. The house belonged to Ray and Doreen Snaith, who lived there with their two sons. The van was a monument to their hope and belief that 'enterprise' might give them an escape from the dole. Ray worked as a steel erector on the night shift at Smith's Dock, and was aged 37 when he was made redundant in August 1986.

The house is their pride and joy – 'It took us two flats and four houses to get here.' Their £23,000 mortgage stretched the family budget to its limits, even though Doreen also had a job for 16 hours a week in a warehouse. So, as soon as Ray discovered he was going to lose his job, he was determined to try to establish a business as a way of raising the money they needed.

The first attempt to enter the 'enterprise culture' came to nothing.

There was a wet fish van that fell through, I missed it by one day. It was dead easy. Go down to Whitby, buy fish, and sell it. He had 500 customers this chap, and he was willing to take me on for a fortnight, and drive me round as proof before any money was handed over, but he wanted £3,000. It was a Sunday, and I was going to borrow the £3,000 on the strength of my redundancy money from my stepmother and one of my mates. But somebody came down from Newcastle on the Sunday night, and gave him cash. We couldn't get to the bank because it was a Sunday.

Ray left with a redundancy pay off of £5,500 and, in spite of missing out on the wet fish van, he soon found another way of investing it.

I knew £5,500 in my pocket wouldn't last long, because I know of other people. They get their redundancy money, and it doesn't last long at all. We were all just talking about it in the cabin, the day we went to pick up our cheques, and somebody said 'There's a fish and

chip van for sale, one of the lads over there's selling one of his
vans.' So I just went over and talked to him, and then I bought it.
I didn't know him to go out drinking with, I just knew him as a
workmate. He had two vans, and he was buying a fish and chip
shop himself. He sold me the van on the understanding that the
trade needed building up again. It used to do a pub in Pallister Park
(in east Middlesbrough), and he said it needed building up again.

The other spot that Ray inherited was a pitch outside a school at
Marton, selling to the children at lunch time. Those few miles he had
to travel from New Marske made it a long working day.

I'd get up and see the kids off to school, and get the van all ready for
around half past ten, and I'd set off about a quarter to eleven.
Sometimes I had to collect my chips on the way. You see you've got
to collect your chips from day to day, sometimes every two days,
depending how many you've got left from the night before.
Then I'd start frying about twenty to twelve. When I got home,
I'd clean up again till about half past two or quarter to three. Or
sometimes it was later because I had to nip down the cash and
carry. Then I'd finished, and I'd start again at about six o'clock. I
used to go about half seven, quarter to eight at one point, but when
I got there it was too early, nobody was buying. So I started going
about a quarter to nine.
Finish at the pub would be about a quarter past eleven. Then I'd
have more cleaning up to do, because you sell more on a night time.
You only have chip butties on with kids, you're not frying fish. On
a night time, it's things like jumbo sausages, fritters, fish and chips,
hamburgers, hot dogs, curry. By the time I'd finished cleaning up,
it'd be about a quarter to twelve, and I did two night clubs Friday
and Saturday. So I'd get there roundabout twenty past, half past
twelve, and they'd come out about two o'clock time, and you
knock off about three o'clock. So it was about a quarter to four
time, when you'd cleaned up there again. Then you count up your
money and go to bed. Start again the next day. When you've been
to a night club, you've got to give it more of a clean. There's more
of a mess because fat gets all over the floor and everything. You
haven't got time to clean in between, especially when you start
serving.

Not only did the business require effort, it also called for a sense of
humour.

You're not supposed to drive a van with hot fat, but these were like big deep fries, and you had a special lid to go over the top, so if it splashes about, it just hits the top of these special pans, but I didn't have the lids. I was still all right. You could do about 30 miles an hour, but that's all the van would do anyway. So we used to switch it on about five miles before you got there, so it was just nice and warm when you pulled up.

When we first started, we went over a level crossing, and my wife was stood up behind me, or I should say she was sliding behind me after we went over the railway lines. All the dripping I'd put in, it all went all over the brand new lino, everywhere. It was the first and last time my wife came out with me. Once it hits the floor of the wagon, it gets all over the place, and while she was serving she was sliding all over. But we were pushing for time, with all the kids coming out. We didn't have time to get it all cleaned up, we just had to stand amongst it.

Ray received only minimal advice and help on his entry into the world of small business.

I went to BSEL to try and get some money off them, but because it was a going concern, they weren't interested. The lad who sold me the van, I had about ten days with him on his other van, just learning how to fry, which was pretty easy, honestly. It cost £2,200 for the van, and I spent a few hundred doing it up. The rest of my redundancy just went keeping the van going, and living off what was left as well, because you never got enough money off the dole.

The engine broke down after the first week. It cost about £50 to get it fixed, and I was off for a fortnight. So I built some new units to put inside – new counters and that. But the petrol consumption was no good – it was petrol, not diesel. Eleven miles to the gallon. And it's about 15 miles to Marton, and it's about 12 to the pub – which is 54 miles. The night club, that's more obviously.

Worse than that, though, the pitches were a major disappointment.

There were two schools together, and it wasn't worth my journey down there. It was no good at all. I might've made about £5 – it wasn't worth the hassle of going there, but I just kept going, hoping it would pick up, but it didn't. I tried other places, but every time I tried a new spot, the takings weren't very good. I always kept going back to the same place in Pallister Park, but it never built up for over two and a half months. I even got a night club – I found that myself – on a Friday and Saturday night, but there was already vans on that site. Hot dog van, kebab van, and me last – and that didn't pull enough money in to keep me going.

It was a very long day. I was paying my nephew £6 a night to help me. My petrol was coming to about £4 a night, but then you've got all your fish, your dripping and everything. With the school, the pub, and the night club, I might've come home with twenty quid, which was just ridiculous. Yet I still did it.

The pub wasn't doing well at all, so I tried one in Guisborough [a fairly prosperous market town about seven miles from Middlesbrough]. The takings was £8. Now it must have cost me £2.50 in petrol. I was supposed to give my nephew £6. He didn't take the £6, so I just gave him three quid. So I've got £2.50 left, and I've used a few buns. I've used dripping, gas, and my petrol. I was out of pocket that particular night. They all just walked past me, but I didn't give up.

I got a pitch at a car boot sale, but there was a hamburger stall about twenty yards from me. Well, that cuts your takings in half straight away. I had hamburgers too. I got my nephew to spy on their prices, and I cut mine five pence lower, but even that didn't work. There was one night they put the clocks back, so they kept the night club open an extra hour. It was hectic that night. The hot dog van went away first, then the kebab van went, and there was only me left, and I sold everything. I actually made about £50 that night.

That night, though, was the only triumphant moment in Ray's business career.

I ran the van for three months. Sometimes my bill for the fisherman was about £180. (If any fish was going off I used to give it to the next door neighbour. He's got 13 cats, so my waste wasn't wasted.) I paid my buns man everyday. What my wife earned part time, we had to put towards the business. I'd work a full week, and I'd be £20 out of pocket. I did seven nights a week until I stopped Wednesdays, that was the worst night of the week. So I worked all them hours, and I didn't make no money.

I couldn't tell you to begin with what was going out and what was coming in. Then eventually we had no money to put towards it, so I knew exactly what was coming in, and I knew I was skint at the end of the week. I was flogging a dead horse. The lad who sold me the van, he offered to sell me a pitch for £2,000. I said, 'Where am I going to get £2,000 from?'

Ray's wife, Doreen, was equally baffled when she saw the business running inexorably downhill. 'It took us a while to work out what we were paying out, because of never being in business before. We just had all this money in a jar. The last week he was going out, I just wanted to say, "Don't go, you're wasting your time." '
'Fancy getting £5,500 in August, and being skint by Christmas,' said Ray. 'It just annoys me, because we got nothing for the house.' This does not rankle with Doreen, though. 'I said, "What's the use of having a new kitchen and a new bathroom, with no money and no job?" If we hadn't bought it, we'd never have known. We'd just have been thinking: "If only we'd bought that fish and chip van, we might've been rolling in it by now." '
Ray too takes a philosophical view.

I've nothing against the lad I bought it off. It just didn't work. He said it needs building up, fair enough, but it should build up after three months. It's a loss, and that's it. It was a gamble. The money would have went anyway. I would've gone out drinking or something. They all do.

There was a momentary idea of trying to convert the van into a mobile video library, then Ray, once bitten twice shy, tried a little elementary market research.

I considered it. It didn't take me long before I unconsidered it. I went out one day all dressed up and everything, and I was going to call house to house to see either VHS or Beta, and plan it out from there, but I went into the shops on the route, and every shop I went into had videos. I went into one, I counted 400 on the shelves. It's all competition. It was a waste of time. What I learned from the fish and chip van was I don't want competition at all.

So instead of being converted into a travelling video shop, the van had to go.

The MOT ran out in January. I advertised it – spent 20 odd quid, couldn't sell it. The tax ran out. So I just left it for a few months, then we advertised it again. It was 12 months later when we sold the van. I lost £500 on the sale of it. I paid £2,200, and I got £1,700.

It may sound a sobering tale, but reassuringly for those who bank on the 'enterprise culture' to be Britain's salvation, Ray would do it all again, if only he had the money. 'I would go into business again, if I had the money and if I had the round. But I don't know whether I'd ever have the chance again, unless I win the pools.'

CHAPTER 13

WORKING AWAY

The little 'uns couldn't understand
where he'd gone.
(Christine Gatley)

We have examined two of the favourite Thatcherite remedies for unemployment, inducing those out of work to acquire new skills, or enticing them into the 'enterprise culture'. A third prescription was 'getting on your bike', though the phrase originated from a remark by Norman Tebbit. This meant that the unemployed should take note of the fact that there were some areas of the country where jobs were much more plentiful than on Teesside, and that they should be prepared to move there.

For those who were willing to consider this option, there were two possibilities. One was to move away from Teesside altogether. The other was to leave the rest of the family behind, take 'digs' in the area where the job was located, and travel home for the weekend, or whenever the job allowed you to get away. The proportion of our interviewees who said they would be prepared to move away from the area remained fairly constant at just over 40 per cent. However, when people were asked whether they *expected* to move away from the area, only 10 per cent said they did, while 78 per cent strongly expected to stay.

Working away, while leaving the family behind, is a well-established tradition on Teesside, alluded to by local MP James Tinn in the parliamentary debate on the closure of Smith's Dock described in chapter 2. The proportion of our interviewees who said they would be prepared to take this option, if necessary, was much higher, generally running at 70 per cent or over.

In the summer of 1988, we tackled the question in a different way, asking the unemployed how far they would be prepared to travel to work. Fourteen per cent said that they would go anywhere in the world, and a further 11 per cent said they would go anywhere in this country. The remainder were prepared to travel up to 50 miles, though 26 per cent were not prepared to go more than 10 miles. These figures suggest rather less enthusiasm for the idea of leaving the family behind and taking a job away from Teesside.

None the less, there is plenty of evidence of people actively chasing jobs outside the area. In the summer of 1987, for instance, 21 people reported having had interviews for jobs in the previous two months, nine of which were outside the county of Cleveland.

Moving away and working away, though, both involve considerable difficulties, especially for those with families. The main problem about moving away, apart from the upheaval it causes, particularly if there is a partner working or children at school, is finding accommodation in another part of the country. For the owner-occupiers who formed the majority of our sample, the major difficulty was that areas that have more jobs also tend to have more expensive houses. House prices on Teesside are lower than in most other parts of England, and the gap between Teesside and the South is enormous. (In the autumn of 1988, building society figures put the average price of a house in Middlesbrough at £35,000, compared with £61,000 nationally, and £100,000 in London.) For council house tenants, there is the problem of finding a tenant from another part of the country who wants to move into Teesside, in order to arrange a swap.

Working away has the obvious emotional and practical difficulties involved in separating one member of the family from the rest for most of the time. There is also the strain and cost of undertaking long journeys at the beginning and end of each period of work, and, in addition, there can be considerable financial problems involved in having to pay for 'digs' near the place of work, which may be in a fairly expensive part of the country, as well as continuing to keep up a home on Teesside.

Another factor that made for a reluctance to move was a genuine affection for the area. Teesside's 'image' has tended to be one of grim heavy industry and pollution, but, in fact, the area surrounding the conurbation contains some very attractive countryside, and the sea is also very close. Nor does Teesside have the problems of traffic congestion and frantic pace of life suffered by the South-east in particular. In the autumn of 1987, we asked people what they liked about Teesside. The vast majority said that it was home or that friends and family were there but there was also a significant minority who said they liked it most for its countryside. Comparatively few said there was nothing much that they liked about the area.

Table 41 *What interviewees liked about Teesside*

	%
It is home/friends and family are here	62
The countryside	10
A friendly place with friendly people	9
Good facilities (e.g. schools)	2
Hard to say (haven't been anywhere else)	2
Nothing/not much	12

Throughout the study, we kept a tally of where in the country were the jobs that people had found. By the autumn of 1988, we found that 10 per cent were commuting daily to a job outside Cleveland, generally meaning a journey of at least 15 miles. A further 8 per cent were working away from home, but only 4 per cent of our sample had actually moved their family home away from Teesside.

Case study

This continues the story of Steve Gatley, begun in the previous chapter.

After the transmission of the 'Shutdown' documentary in February 1988, Steve Gatley was offered a job. That was the good news. The bad news was that to take it, he would have to leave his family behind on Teesside. The job he was offered was to run a fish and chip shop at Aylesbury in Buckinghamshire, more than 200 miles from his home at Billingham. The offer came from a viewer of the programme who owned a chain of fish and chip shops, and who had been impressed by what he saw as Steve's dedication and determination.

So on the Easter Weekend of 1988, Steve left Christine and the four children behind, and set off for the South. When I went to see Steve, he had been away from home for a month. The chip shop was on a big council estate. Steve's living quarters were a small room off the back of the shop. He slept on a fold-up bed. There was no bath. The previous Christmas he had taken the view that working away was the only realistic option. He said he had done it before, and he was fairly blasé about the effect it would have on him. Now, though, was he missing the family more than he had expected?

You're too busy to miss home actually, especially when I first started. It's a hard job I've got now, it's the hardest one I've ever had. It's very demanding. I work 14 hours a day, including the preparation, but I'm used to it. I don't mind the work now.

I get up between 7 and 7.30. I do potatoes, usually four or five hundred pounds in the machine. And I eye them by hand, then I chip them. After that I'll polish the shopware, and I'll bone approximately two to three, maybe four stone of fish a day, and I rub all the range down, I mop up, and I sweep up, and I have half an hour to read a paper.

Then I get everything prepared such as pies and pasties and the chickens ready to be heated up in the microwave to go into the actual range, and then, by the time I've done that, it's time to put the pans on and start frying. I open at half eleven, then we close at quarter to two. Then the next time we open is half four, but I start work approximately quarter past, half past three, because there's usually chickens to barbecue, and there's usually more fish to bone for the following day which I do to try and get in front.

We open up at half four, close at ten o'clock. I get some of the staff, if we have enough time, to clean up. I cash up in the till, put all the money right, but during the day we have people coming in with supplies, and I have to pay them as well, and it's a bit of a rush when we have a shop full of people, and the supplies are coming in at the same time. Then at the end of the night, if there's any chickens left, I barbecue them ready for tomorrow morning, and it's the same over and over again, apart from Thursday and Friday which are the busiest days.

At night I pack up about half ten, quarter to eleven. That's after I've cashed up, checked everything's off. When I've had a wash, I get to bed about five past, ten past eleven. Then I'm up again at half past seven, and the same again for six days a week.

On a Saturday night we close at ten. I ask the staff to stay back an extra ten minutes so they can mop up, while I cash up. Saturday afternoon during the half hour I have off, I nip down for some petrol. About half past ten, I check everything's off, I lock the shutters. I jump in my car, and I get home about half two, three o'clock in the morning. As soon as I get home, I have a nice hot bath, straight to bed, and I'm up again at eight or nine o'clock in the morning, say hello to the kids, take them out for the day.

Then I come home or maybe go out for a few pints, and go back to bed. Get up between three and half past three in the morning, have a cup of coffee, travel down four o'clock in the morning, and get here for nine o'clock. I drive about 10 hours out of thirty-five, because I have about 35 hours to myself from Saturday night to Monday morning.

Steve's gross pay was around £450 a week, but out of that he had to pay his staff, leaving him about £250, and out of that, his petrol cost £40 a week. Still, it was a good deal more than he was earning at Smith's Dock, and it was helping him to clear the debts he had accumulated while he was running his own fish and chip shop.

I've paid a lot of bills actually. I've told the boss why I'm here – money and money only, but I need it so I have to work away. I've no choice. The bad things are that I miss the family. I don't have any freedom at all when I'm in here, because the job's too demanding, but I'm used to it, and I don't mind it now. I just miss the children. The money down here, with the hours I do, it's OK, it's not bad at all. I'm on a contract for six months here. I'd gladly last that six months, but Christine doesn't want me down here.

Steve was conscious that, back in Billingham, Christine was finding life very hard.

She has the four children by herself now. Sometimes she 'phones me on a night time, and tells me she just can't cope, because of the four youngsters. They play up a lot with me not being there, they do a lot of fighting and carrying on. When I'm home they make a fuss of me, which I like anyway. I can't keep my eye on them all the time, and the day I'm off, I don't want to chastise them or tell them off, I just want to be loving and caring with them.

Steve's contract was for six months, at the end of which he would be entitled to a bonus, and he would also have the chance to buy or rent the shop, but already he was beginning to wonder whether he would be able to stick it out.

I could, but I don't think Chris could. I don't think she could handle me working away all the time. She's asked me to come home now actually.

There's a lot of money to be made down here. It's a place to have a fish shop, if I did buy one, we'd probably have to move down here. It's no good having your family somewhere different from

where your shop is. It's too far to travel. Chris has lived all over, so
I don't think she would mind. Her mother lives in London.

There isn't many fish shops down here. I've only ever seen two in
Aylesbury, and there's a lot of houses, and they're being built all
the time right next to each other. They never stop building houses
here. So this shop is fairly busy. Thursday and Friday nights it
never stops for two hours solid, three hours sometimes. But up
north it's not so good. Everybody in this area – Aylesbury – is
working, so they've got the money to spend on fish and chips.
Whereas at Port Clarence, there wasn't much employment there, it
was all unemployment.

I've seen nothing at all of Aylesbury. I just go to the rubbish
dump three times a week, and that's the only time I see daylight. I
get on fine with the customers. They talk nice to me. I've made a
few good friends. I've had trouble with my car, and a lad who
comes in, took my car and helped fix it for me. It's been smashing,
they've helped me out, told me where the bank and that is, and
where to get cheap petrol from. I get on very well with the staff, I've
got very good staff.

Even though Steve had been virtually confined to the shop during
his brief stay in Aylesbury, he had seen enough to reach his own
conclusions about whether Britain had a North-South divide:

Definitely. Every car that pulls up outside this fish shop, if it's
below an 'A' reg you might as well forget about it, because they're
all A,B,C,D and E ['E' was the latest registration at this time]. You
can definitely tell there's a North-South divide. You can tell this is
an all-Tory area, because of the cars they drive and the money they
spend in this place.

You can pick and choose what job you want down here, whereas
up north they pick and choose you, and you have no say in the
matter, but down here, you can do anything, because there's that
many vacancies for jobs.

When Steve first went south, he had a week in the shop with the
owner, but now relations were not as happy. Steve had asked for three
weeks off to help Christine with the children, as his youngest son was
about to go into hospital. The owner replied that it was Steve's
responsibility to cover for any absences, and that though he would
come up from Cornwall himself to cover on this occasion, he would

not expect to have to do it again, and that Steve would lose money. Steve had been rather depressed by this development.

I am a bit disappointed. I thought the boss'd treat me a bit better, but he wrote me a letter which I didn't like. I work quite hard for him, and I shut half an hour early on a Saturday night, so I could cash up and clean up, and he didn't like it, so he told me. And I didn't like the way he put it over, because he knows I have to travel all the way up north, and I didn't think half an hour would hurt. It's a good job, I like it. I've had a bit of a tiff with the boss, that's all.

In the event, Steve's boss not only covered for him while his son had his operation, he also offered to do so again to allow Steve some time with his family. 'He said he'd cover for me, and he said I could take three weeks' holiday in July, and he'd cover for me then.'

While he was at home, though, Steve took the opportunity to look for work locally, chasing jobs as a plater or as a driver, but he was unsuccessful. So he went back to the chip shop at Aylesbury. A week later, he came home for his few stolen Sunday hours with his family. Christine takes up the story:

He came home on the Sunday, and we had a talk about it, and the Monday morning he was going back, and I said, 'I don't want you to go', and he said, 'Oh, I'll have to, I'll have to'. Anyway, he went back and 'phoned me when he got there, because he always 'phoned me as soon as he got there.

So the 'phone went to let me know he'd arrived, and he said, 'Chris, I can't handle it', and I said, 'Please come home, will you come home?' And he said, 'I don't know, I can't just walk out, I've just come back.' Anyway, he had a talk to his boss, and he knew that, with Steve having a family, he'd miss us as well as we do him. So he arrived home, and it was a relief. It was great.

Steve, however, saw the difficulties.

The first feeling was, 'Will I get another job at home?' You see, I knew how difficult it was to get a job, and it was worrying me all the way driving home. That's all I could think about for four hours. So when I got home, I told her, 'I might be out of a job.' She said that's OK, as long as I'm home.

For a fortnight, Steve's fears seemed to be justified. He could not find work. Christine began to get depressed, and even started to regret that he had left Aylesbury. Then Steve found a job in Billingham, back at his old trade of plating. After two weeks there, he was laid off again, but the following day, he found another plating job, though the circumstances illustrated the extent to which the Teesside job scene had become casualised. Steve was not directly employed. Instead he signed up with an agency, which then hired him out to a company that had vacancies for platers.

After all this time, getting back into plating, it's been hard, but where I am now, we do chassis and large trucks and fork-lifts. All the lads stick together, all the fabricators, that's what we're known as now. See, I was a bit rusty, and all the lads have been helping me out on different jobs. All you have to do is ask a question and they'll show you how to do something. I like the place where I work. It's a nice clean area, clean shop.

What had been distilled, though, from the experience of having Steve working away? Christine could find little to recommend it:

It was terrible. When he went back on Monday, tears – the kids missed him. The kids started fretting. They knew I was upset, and when you're upset, the kids are upset. We used to 'phone each other up twice a day, but I couldn't stand it. It's very hard especially for the children.

The little 'uns couldn't understand where he'd gone. They'd think he'd just gone to work, but when he'd come on the 'phone, they'd say, 'Where are you Dad, are you coming home?' All right, we needed the money, because we do have debt, but money isn't everything. I was trying to be a mum and a dad to them, which is very hard to do. They wanted things all the time. When Steve was at home, he could say, 'You're not getting this, you're not getting that', but if I said 'no' they used to play me up. They'd cry for things all the time, but I used to give in to them. It's like you can't control them yourself, you do need a man there with you.

It's great now because he's coming home to us, that's something to look forward to now. He comes in and they jump on him. Have his tea ready, and he's there with you all night with the kids. The kids see more of him, especially the baby. He needs his dad there with him.

Steve looked at it slightly differently.

I enjoyed it at first. It was good money, but it was hard work. But I didn't mind the hard work. I'd work away again if I could have holidays. I wouldn't mind working two weeks on, one week off; or three weeks on, one week off. I wouldn't mind anything like that, as long as I can have time at home.

The idea of Steve's ever working away again at first horrified Christine, though she too felt it might be bearable if he could have longer intervals at home. 'I'd go with him. I'd get in the suitcase! No, I couldn't go through all that again. It would be all right if he went away for a fortnight, and could come home for a fortnight, but that one day wasn't enough. It wasn't enough at all.'

The failure of his business, the accumulated debt of £6,000 that it left him, and the unhappy experience of working away had done nothing to dim Steve's optimism and determination. He had his heart set on starting another business.

I miss the challenge. It's all right your nine to five sort of thing, but after five o'clock you have no responsibilities. You're just home, and that's it, but, having your own business, it's on you 24 hours a day. That's what I like. I plan to do it again.

I'll get another business. I don't know what, but I know for a fact I will. I've got another three years to pay my debts off, and that's me cleared, if I can keep this job, and after that I can start banking money and saving it. Plus, the car I've got, I got that for another business actually. I was going to go for a taxi business, but I didn't have the finances, so I've got to keep this job to pay for the car, and my other debts. But I decided with Chris the other day that I'm going to let her take lessons, and she can drive as well, so that will help me in the future.

The fish and chip shop business gave me a lot of experience. People have pulled me up in the street, and said I was a fool to take it on, I've lost all my money, I was foolish. But for me, at least I've tried something. I've lost a lot of money, yes, but I've got the experience. Not many people my age would have done that. I did everything right with the fish and chip shop. I did all the market research and everything, and I'll do the same again.

I'll definitely go in business again. I like the challenge. I panicked the first time, I was mixed up a little, but the determination was there. Personally, I succeeded. It wasn't my fault the business flopped, it wasn't through lack of trying.

Christine, as before, was less enthusiastic about the idea of starting a new business.

He's had a big let-down and everything, but it was a lot of strain, especially on me and the children. When you've got your own business, it is a lot of worry. He had a lot of things on his mind. He used to come home, and I used to get it all, and the kids used to be there. It's very very hard, and we were on the verge of splitting up.

He'd like to go into business again. I wouldn't like him to go into business again, but it depends on the way it's going to work out. He's learned his lesson in one way. I mean he'll never go rushing to get anything like that again. He'll think seriously about what he does now. This job he's got now, he goes out to work in the morning, he comes home at night. He has no worries. None whatsoever.

CHAPTER 14

COUNTING THE COST

What can I do? They closed my
shipyard. I've lost my job.
(Ian Dale)

The purpose of this book was not to question whether or not Smith's Dock should have been closed. It may well be that we simply cannot afford to prop up our old traditional industries, and that to attempt to do so would just be to throw good money after bad, though it is interesting to note that some observers are now claiming to see the first signs of an upturn in world shipbuilding.

The problem is that a willingness to take painful decisions of this kind has often been coupled with an unwillingness to recognise just how painful the consequences are going to be for those on the receiving end. How much easier, after all, to gain acceptance of such decisions if you can persuade yourself that they have no real victims. It is my belief that our research has demonstrated that such sentiments are an illusion. Even if you believe it was right to close Smith's Dock, you surely owe it to those thrown out of work not to minimise or misrepresent their ordeal.

It appears to be a trait of human nature to regard those out of work as idle. In this case it is demonstrably untrue and unfair. The 23 per cent of Smith's Dock workers who had no job in the summer of 1988 were not out of work because they were idle. They were out of work because the Government, rightly or wrongly, had closed their shipyard.

In fact, what is striking is the opposite of idleness, namely, people's extraordinary determination to find work – persistently visiting job centres that had no suitable vacancies on offer, writing endless letters to employers who did not answer. Even those close to retiring age were reluctant to call it a day. As these pages have shown, there were wives prepared to work for £4 a week, men prepared to work away from their families month after month. Many of the unemployed said they would take any job; most were asking for just £100 a week or less.

Other findings of the research have thrown into question whether money is the main motive for wanting to work at all. It is certainly clear that there are other powerful pressures, like the need to feel useful, to have an aim in life, to enjoy self-respect, to have a routine to the day, to have an escape route from the home which becomes a prison if you are confined there. Often, above all, having a job simply provides something to do.

This suggests that our obsession with holding down benefits in order to ensure that there is an 'incentive' to work may be pointless, as well as cruel. It is certainly cruel. Three quarters of those in our sample getting benefits say they are not enough to live on. Nearly a fifth of the unemployed cannot afford to buy the food they need. Two-fifths find degrading the process of claiming benefits (for which they had paid in taxation and national insurance contributions while they were in work).

When you read about the hardships undergone by those made redundant at Smith's Dock, you have to remind yourself that, compared with the rest of the unemployed, this was actually a *favoured* group. Their redundancy terms were a great deal more generous than the law requires, and more favourable than many people receive.

Apart from being cruel, the benefits system appears to have been constructed without understanding of the realities of the labour market. Its complexity makes signing on and off daunting, and yet that is precisely what Cleveland's casualised labour market – casualised in line with Government thinking about making it more 'flexible' – required many workers to do. In addition, there are features that constitute an actual disincentive to work, like allowing a wife to earn only £4 a week if her husband was on supplementary benefit, and reducing the help towards mortgage interest payments in the first months of unemployment.

There was a high degree of cynicism about those official agencies with which the unemployed had contact, whether these were the benefit authorities or those supposed to 'help' unemployed people find work. This probably resulted as much as anything from the strong scent of penny-pinching that attached to them. A Government that was never very keen on public spending of any description seemed to be always going for things on the cheap. This was most notable in the new ET (Employment Training) scheme where 'trainees' were to be paid their dole money plus £10 a week. As far as the benefits system went, many had the suspicion that its intricacies and poor communications were designed to ensure that everyone did *not* claim everything they were entitled to, as this too saved money.

Nor can we as a society fall back on the excuse of shortage of funds for all this. Our Government has money coming out of its ears. That is why it is particularly shocking to hear of incidents like Josie O'Marra's being told to pay her own bus fare to her Re-start interview the day after the Chancellor has given away billions of pounds to the top earners.

Attempts to help find work for former Smith's Dock employees was limited, first by money – not much was provided; and second by ideology – nothing could be done to create new jobs specifically for those made redundant, as this would interfere with market forces. Instead, people would be offered appropriately Thatcherite self-help remedies – re-training, enterprise or relentless job-searching.

Many were re-trained, and most seemed satisfied with the quality of their courses. But how much effort went into finding out what skills were in demand in the local economy, and what, therefore, people should be trained in? None that I am aware of, and, if there was any, it was clearly deficient, as only a third of those who went on a course said it helped to find them a job.

Enterprise was tried by a handful of low-investment, low-tech ventures, but the degree of enthusiasm with which this most Thatcherite of responses was embraced is called into considerable doubt. Most of those who set up their own business said they would give it up if someone offered them a job. Relentless searching could be done through job clubs, but it is important to remember that job clubs do not create jobs. They set out to offer their members a better chance of getting one of the scarce jobs already on offer, at the expense of others who are out of work. Even on these terms, they worked for only a pitifully small number of our sample.

Still, people did get jobs. At the time of writing, two-thirds of those made redundant have now got new jobs, but, 18 months after the closure, more than a fifth have not. This means that the labour market still had not absorbed the shock of Smith's Dock's closure, and that unemployment is still higher than it would otherwise be in an area where it was already high enough.

Furthermore, the rate of job finding among our sample should not be seen as typical of the unemployed as a whole. Again, you have to bear in mind that the former Smith's Dock workforce was a favoured group among unemployed people. BSEL may have had its deficiencies, but at least it was an agency of some sort, specially dedicated to helping those put out of work to find jobs. That was more than the rest of the unemployed on Teesside got.

As for the kind of jobs people got, many demanded very long working hours, were even worse paid than Smith's Dock, and, above all, were casual and insecure. (One of the ironies of this was that the very changes the Government promoted in the labour market, like casualisation, lowering wages, breaking trade union power, all tended to encourage the growth of the Black Economy, on which it was committed to cracking down.) A few found the closure showed them new horizons they would probably never have glimpsed had the yard stayed open, but it was only a few.

More than a year after Smith's Dock closed, we asked our interviewees themselves to count the cost. Three quarters said that for them personally the closure had been a bad thing. Only 16 per cent said it had opened up new possibilities, or that they had found a better job.

We seem to consider that the unemployed forfeit many of their rights as human beings when they lose their jobs. We tend not to seek their opinions on the 'services' they are offered in terms of job-finding or benefits, and yet their views would surely be the most illuminating. In our research we tried to remedy some of these omissions, asking what could be done to make unemployment more bearable, or claiming benefits less degrading.

One of the most obvious and basic problems that emerged was lack of information. It was sobering to learn that comparatively few of the unemployed had heard even of the very limited concessionary schemes that were available to them. Perhaps it is time that we introduced pre-redundancy courses, just as many employers have pre-retirement courses, for those about to lose their jobs. These would cover how to cope with the emotional traumas, how to develop new interests, what cheap or free activities there are, how to get all the benefits you are entitled to, and how to make ends meet.

Alas, instituting such an idea would take considerable political courage. At the moment, virtually all the help that is given to the unemployed is conditioned by the idea that the normal human state is to be in work, and that soon they will have returned to it. Actually teaching people to cope with unemployment would be a recognition that the state of the labour market is such that many will be without work for a prolonged period. Nevertheless, in all humanity, the pill must be swallowed. A great deal can, and, therefore, must be done to make unemployment more bearable. To reiterate a crucial point –

you can believe that re-structuring the economy by closing places like Smith's Dock is essential, but also believe that those made unemployed should be treated a great deal better. Indeed, if the unemployed were treated better, the effect would be to make such changes more acceptable.

Too often we tell ourselves that it is not really so bad for them, because there are plenty of jobs for those who really want to work, or because the dole is really quite comfortable, or because those who once worked suddenly become lazy and shiftless in our eyes when they are sacked through no fault of their own. All of this might be an understandable reaction. After all, those of us who are in work and comfortably off often do feel a sense of guilt when we see others thrown on the scrapheap.

'To give a voice to those who have no voice.' That was the aim of this book. And what that voice tells us is that the closure of a workplace is a tragedy for those who work there. It may be necessary as part of some macro-economic plan, but, at least, let us pay those who have lost their jobs the courtesy of recognising what they have suffered.

But they are entitled to something more – more compassion, more understanding, and, above all, more resourceful and imaginative assistance than is to be found in the story of those who were made redundant when Smith's Dock shut down.

CHAPTER 15

POSTSCRIPT

As we approach the second anniversary of Smith's Dock's closure, there are signs that things might be looking up on Teesside. The County of Cleveland has lost its uncoveted position at the top of the unemployment league to Merseyside (though it is still in second place, with a rate of more than 15 per cent) and the Government is putting money into reviving the area.

In the afterglow of her 1987 general election victory, the Prime Minister had discovered a mission to revive the inner cities. After proclaiming it from Downing Street, she visited some of the places in need of revival. First stop was Teesside, where Mrs Thatcher was bold enough to be photographed against the background of a derelict site. These are not hard to find – Teesside has the dubious distinction of containing the biggest area of industrial dereliction in Europe. There was a good deal of cynicism about her visit from some of those who used to have jobs before dereliction replaced factories, notably from an unemployed man who waved his one thousand unsuccessful job applications under the Prime Minister's nose.

However, the good news from Teesside's point of view was that the visit had made the area high profile. There was clearly going to be a great deal of political capital staked on ensuring that the derelict site against which the Prime Minister had been photographed was no longer derelict by the time of the next general election. To try to achieve this end, the Government has put an urban development corporation on Teesside. These bodies are given a great deal of public money to repair the infrastructure and powers to by-pass local authority planning regulations, with the ultimate aim of attracting private sector investment to decaying areas.

Teesside Development Corporation is by far the biggest in the country, and has been given £160 million to spend over seven years. An energetic team was put to work in the autumn of 1987.

Achievements on job creation have so far been modest. A year after it began work, the Corporation claimed to have created or 'protected' just 700 jobs. However, it also claimed to have been the catalyst in initiating a number of important new ventures – these included the European Chemical Centre, said to be the finest concentration of chemical businesses in the world; a massive new retail, sports and leisure complex at the old Stockton racecourse; a motor sport park; and, probably the star of the show so far, the Tees Offshore Base.

This has been developed in association with the Tees and Hartlepool Port Authority on the old Smith's Dock site. It can be credited with 450 of those 700 jobs created or saved by the Development Corporation. The base is designed to attract businesses that are involved with the North Sea. Among those who have come are a Norwegian company operating offshore support vessels, a Dutch company which moved its shipping agency office from the centre of Middlesbrough, and British Telecom Marine which brought its cable-laying ships. Most of these ventures did not offer much hope of employment to former Smith's Dock workers, but one company did. It was called Tees Dockyard, and it took over the old dry docks, which had been closed down in the early 1980s when Smith's Dock pulled out of ship repairing.

The majority of those recruited at Tees Dockyard are former Smith's Dock workers, but ship repairing remains a highly competitive business, and many of those who returned have found that working conditions have changed very significantly. Because the company is having to live from contract to contract, it has not been able to offer the kind of permanent employment that they had been used to at Smith's Dock. The workforce has generally fluctuated between 100 and 200, but at present the so-called 'core workforce' is only 75. For the rest, working life, as in so much of Teesside's industry, means short contracts which can often end very suddenly. The latest forecast is that by the end of 1990, the Tees Offshore Base will employ a thousand people, though in late 1988, it took rather a blow when British Telecom announced that it was going to pull its ships out.

So there are signs of a much-needed revival on Teesside, but as far as shipbuilding goes, the news, in Britain at least, seems to get worse and worse. In the autumn of 1988, there were reports that the long-awaited upturn in world shipbuilding was at last going to happen. Lloyd's Register noted that there had been an increase of three quarters of a million tons in the amount of shipping on order or being built. Other authorities claimed that sea trade was growing, that there were fewer ships laid up, and that the prices for new and second-hand ships had begun to rise again after years of stagnation, though sceptics would point out that the upturn has allegedly been just round the corner for most of the last 15 years.

At the same time, it was revealed that in Britain things were rather different. Our total order book had actually fallen in the first half of 1988, and the size of our merchant fleet had dropped by a staggering 75 per cent during the 1980s, as against a fall of 8 per cent in the rest of the world. Meanwhile, the Government was itching to get British Shipbuilders – seen as the last lame duck nationalised industry – off its hands. The then Industry Minister, Kenneth Clarke, claimed that every job in the group was costing the taxpayer £20,000 a year to preserve.

In Sunderland, 30 miles up the coast from Middlesbrough, more than 2,000 people, a fifth of the total male workforce still work in the town's two shipyards. Overall male unemployment is over 20 per cent, and runs at 40 per cent in some areas around the yards. In addition, it is reckoned that a further 5,000 jobs could be indirectly dependent on shipbuilding. Many of the workers have already been laid off, after a dispute arose between British Shipbuilders and a Danish company over payment for a fleet of ferries that the Danes had ordered.

Then into the story came the Cubans. They said they wanted Sunderland to build 10 cargo ships. On Teesside, the belief was that the Cubans, who had bought ships from Smith's Dock in the past, had really wanted the ships built there, and that, if the yard had not been closed, they would have won the order. Be that as it may, it now looked as though Teesside's loss might be Wearside's gain. The order would be worth £100 million, though the Cubans would be looking for the usual 28 per cent subsidy (see chapter 1) from the British government. Now, though, it seemed this might not be forthcoming. Kenneth Clarke announced: 'I should consider requests for support with considerable scepticism in the light of past losses.' Any such aid was to be conditional on a private buyer being found for the yards.

Offers were investigated, deadlines came and went, but, in the end, it was announced that there was no suitable offer, and the Sunderland yards would close. Even then, there were hopes of a reprieve, with news that the Cubans might be prepared to lease one of the yards to build the ships in, saving 900 of the 2,200 jobs at stake. Meanwhile, the Government is offering a £10 million re-training and business support scheme for workers made redundant from the yard. At the time of writing, the issue remains unresolved, but for those who have followed the story of Smith's Dock, it all has an ominously familiar ring. While this drama was being played out at Sunderland, we carried out two further rounds of interviewing of our sample of Smith's Dock workers. The interviews for Round 9 were done in the autumn of 1988, and for Round 10 around Christmas. As far as the balance between employed and unemployed is concerned, if we compare the results with those shown in table 7 in chapter 4, there is some evidence that the number of former Smith's Dock employees who have been able to find new work may have reached a plateau at around 65 per cent. Similarly, the number unemployed seems now to be stuck at just over 20 per cent, though it is important to point out that well over half of these have had jobs since the yard closed.

Table 42 *Employment status of former Smith's Dock workers*

	Round 9 (%)	Round 10 (%)
Employed	65	63
Unemployed	24	22
In training/education	2	3
Sick/retired	9	12

Many of those in work still had to be content with temporary jobs. In the final round of questioning, 41 per cent of those working full-time were in casual or contract jobs. Once again we asked those who had worked how many jobs they had had since leaving Smith's Dock. The results showed that half the sample had had to do a number of different jobs.

Table 43 *Jobs held by those interviewees who have had work since Smith's Dock closed*

No. of jobs	%
1	50
2	22
3	13
4	5
5	5
6	2
8	2
10	1

We also took a final look at whether the new jobs gave as much satisfaction as those the interviewees had done at Smith's Dock. Here the results were encouraging. When we asked 'Would you say your new job makes more/less/the same use of your talents and skills as your job at Smith's Dock?', 55 per cent said it made more use, against only half as many who said it made less. As far as pay was concerned, though, 30 per cent of those in work said they were getting less than at Smith's Dock. Indeed, more than half of the whole sample (including those in work) said they had less money coming into the household than when they were at the yard.

There were a number of points on which we wanted to get a kind of 'end of term' report. One was whether men or women had been more successful at finding work. The small number of women in the sample means that it is hard to arrive at firm conclusions, but it does appear that they were marginally more successful in the labour market than the men, though nearly half of the women who found work were in part-time jobs. When it comes to the effect of age on success at finding work, however, the conclusions are more clear-cut. Of those under 40, 73 per cent were in work. For those over 40, the figure was only 49 per cent. The unemployment rate for those over 40, though, was not far out of line with the rate for the whole sample. What was significant was that a quarter of those over 45 described themselves as sick or disabled. Still only a tiny handful – less than 4 per cent – of this age group said they were 'retired'. The unemployed were still hunting for work. Nearly two-thirds said they had applied for a job since the job since the last interview, though of those who had been out of work ever since the yard closed, the proportion was only one-third.

In the final round of questioning, we also asked how many jobs people had applied for altogether. Among the unemployed, we found that more than half had applied for over 15 jobs; more than 20 per cent had applied for over 40; and more than 10 per cent for over 60. Those who had applied for very large numbers of jobs, though, seemed more likely to be found among the employed than the unemployed. Nearly 10 per cent of those in work had applied for 100 jobs or more, three times the rate for those unemployed. The result of submitting endless applications was often discouraging. More than 60 per cent of the unemployed said that fewer than half of their applications even produced a reply.

Next, we examined how successful the Government's efforts to help the Smith's Dock workforce find jobs through BSEL had been. Just 11 per cent of the sample said they had got work through BSEL, though 43 per cent said it had helped in other ways; by far the most common form of help quoted was the provision of a training course. As far as training was concerned, nearly half the workforce said they wanted to go on a course when the yard closed, and, of these, the vast majority – 90 per cent – succeeded, though they did not always get the course of their choice. However, when you examine whether the training provided was useful – from the individual's point of view in terms of helping him find work, or from the point of view of the economy as a whole in terms of providing skills that were in short supply – the answer is disappointing. Only 38 per cent of those who were re-trained said that their courses helped them find a job.

BSEL also provided a job club, and there were others in the area. Fewer than 20 per cent of our sample joined one. Of those, just a quarter, seven individuals, said it got them a job. This is well below the two-thirds success rate which is claimed on posters promoting job clubs. Government schemes, like the Community Programme, can provide employment directly for those out of work, but, of our sample, fewer than 6 per cent had actually worked on such schemes. When unemployed interviewees were asked whether they would be prepared to accept a place on the government's new Employment Training (ET) scheme, which has been the subject of such fierce debate, two-thirds said they would not.

Another government scheme, Re-start, is ostensibly designed to help get the long-term unemployed back to work, though critics regard it as a way of frightening them off the register. Of those in our sample who had been to Re-start interviews, three-quarters said they had found them unhelpful, and fewer than 5 per cent said the interview helped them find a job. In most cases, the outcome seemed inconclusive. About a quarter reported that it was suggested they should join a job club, go on a training course, or that job opportunities were suggested to them. One interviewee reported that the discussion had scared him into looking more seriously for work.

Paying basic household bills remained a problem for a small minority of the sample, with 15 per cent saying they had difficulties paying normal family expenses, 9 per cent saying they had trouble with the mortgage, and smaller numbers quoting other household bills. Generally the numbers reporting problems were split about half and half between those employed and those not in work (though the proportion was higher among the unemployed), pointing once again to the poor pay rates in many of the jobs that had been found.

As for the state of mind of those still unemployed two years after the yard's closure, nearly 20 per cent say they do not think they will ever get another job. Indeed, if you take those who have not had a job at all since the yard closed, the figure rises to nearly 40 per cent. The majority of the unemployed say they would not now be prepared to leave the family behind and work away from Teesside, nor would they be prepared to move the family away. As for their view of the future, hope and apprehension were split virtually equally, with 42 per cent saying they were happy or reasonably happy, and 45 per cent saying they were concerned or very concerned.

Finally, what of those whose stories were told in the case studies in this book? Barry Reed, whose experiences are described in chapter 4, is still plagued by his back injury, and is now on invalidity benefit. His younger son, Derek, is on the new Employment Training scheme. Six months after getting his heavy goods driving job, Les Hill found himself out of work again when the company he was working for lost its contract with British Steel. Now, though, after four months of unemployment, Les is about to go back to work with them.

Josie O'Marra's story has taken a turn for the better. One day, she noticed a new optician's shop and, on the off chance, asked whether they were looking for a cleaner. The answer was that they were, and Josie got the job. Now she has just started a second part-time cleaning job, at the doctor's where her elder daughter Patricia works. Her elder son, Michael, is just about to start work with a sub-contractor at British Steel, while her younger son, Stephen, has been back on the dole since his Community Programme job finished in October 1988. Her younger daughter, Joanne, is still at school.

True to his prediction, Roger Spence has not got bored, even though he has stayed in retirement. He has not entirely lost interest in ships and shipbuilding, though. At present, he is chairman of the North-east branch of the Maritime League, which is dedicated to trying to arrest the decline of the British merchant fleet, mentioned earlier in this chapter. Since the end of his story in chapter 8, Tommy Cushley has had no less than three jobs – all of them clerical and with companies involved in the offshore oil industry. He expects the latest one to keep him in work for several more months. Tommy is enjoying clerical work: 'I think I've found my vocation', he says. His wife Lesley now has a part-time job as a barmaid.

In spite of his fears about its insecurity, Ian Dale has kept his job. Linda, his wife, has found it hard to get a job, though she did some temporary work over Christmas, serving in the shop were she used to clean. Dave Waller, who we met in chapter 11, has managed to find a job. He has been at a bridge-building company in Darlington for six months, and is hopeful they may have work for another two years. The Wallers sold their car, and their house, but have managed to buy another one. They have also acquired another daughter.

Then there were our two would-be entrants into the 'enterprise culture'. After more than a year on the dole, Ray Snaith went south, to do a labouring job on a building site in Berkshire. He expected a few weeks' work, but, nine months later, he is still there. The good thing about the job is that there is plenty of overtime, and they have not had to sell their house. The bad thing is that weekend working has restricted his opportunities to get home. His visit at Christmas was the first in four months.

Steve Gatley is still in the same job in which we left him in chapter 13. He still has more than £5,000 to pay off from his ill-fated fish and chip shop venture but, optimistic as ever, he nurtures ambitions of going back into business. His old shop, which he had to sell, is now being re-furbished as the local council plays its part in the regeneration of Teesside.

January 1989

Appendix

NOTE ON RESEARCH METHODS
Shamalah Tucker

The project involved a two-year longitudinal study, in which interviews were conducted every two months in the first year, and every three months in the second year.

A database of employees' names from the payroll list formed the basis for extracting a sample representative of the workforce. The sample was stratified according to the major occupational categories in the yard. Within these strata, interviewees were randomly chosen.

Two groups of workers were not included in the redundancy notification, and were not, therefore, included in the sample. These were the apprentices and the refinery workers. The apprentices were to be found positions elsewhere in British Shipbuilders, or with other local firms. Refinery workers were operating on a contract in a refinery, administration of which was simply passed to another part of British Shipbuilders. In total, the two groups accounted for 125 people.

In order to allow for non-responses, 255 people were selected, with the hope of establishing a sample of 200. Given the length of time that the study would take, it was considered that this would provide a reasonable 'cushion' to allow for people dropping out. The selected individuals were then approached to establish their willingness to take part in the project.

In round one, the number of completed questionnaires returned was 186. To achieve the target of 200 interviewees, an additional group was selected, using the same stratified random technique. The average sample size for the first year was 185, while for the second year, it was 180. After the initial difficulties in establishing a large enough sample, the 'drop-out' rate was small. The dates for the interview rounds are showing in the Introduction.

For each round of interviewing, a questionnaire consisting of structured and unstructured questions was agreed by the Polytechnic and representatives of Thames Television. To measure changes over time, a number of questions were repeated at specific intervals. Briefing and de-briefing sessions were held at the beginning and end of each round of interviews.

At the briefing sessions, the questionnaires were discussed by members of the project team and the interviewers to ensure that they were clear and sufficiently comprehensive. Profile sheets were issued for recording additional informations given by the interviewee, or considered to be of significance by the interviewer, but not covered by the questionnaire. Thames also requested that the interviewers and the project team should be aware of individuals who might make a useful contribution to the television documentaries being produced. Those who proved to be of interest were then approached to see if they would be willing to be contacted by Thames.

At debriefing sessions, the focus was on the problems faced by interviewers, and potential matters of interest for future rounds. Thames representatives attended these debriefings to discuss the future direction of the research, and possible candidates for filming.

Following the collection of the questionnaires, the structured questions were coded and entered into a computer. A print-out was produced which was verified against the individual questionnaires to remove any errors before analysis was performed, using a statistical package known as SPSS^X (Statistical Package for Social Science). The more qualitative aspects of the research were hand-analysed. A report was prepared at the end of each round for Thames, highlighting the major findings.

Some of the areas that we were investigating involved sensitive personal issues, and needed skilled handling. Each interviewer continued, wherever possible, with the same group of interviewees. This meant that, over a number of rounds, a *rapport* could be built up, allowing the introduction of more sensitive questions. On two occasions, spouses/partners of the respondents were interviewed separately.

A 'quality check' was carried out in December 1987 on the entire workforce made redundant at Smith's Dock. The purpose of this check was to ensure that the results being obtained from the sample were, indeed, representative of the entire workforce. It consisted of a short postal questionnaire, inquiring about people's employment status, followed up by telephone calls and, if necessary, a visit.

This produced 814 responses. The results, compared with the figures derived from the sample at that time, were:

	Sample	Postal questionnaire
In work	40%	43%
Unemployed	38%	37%
In training/education	12%	12%
Sick or retired	7%	7%

Just published

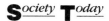

Walter Schwarz

The New Dissenters:
The Nonconformist Conscience in the Age of Thatcher

'The new Dissenters are the heirs of the Nonconformist Conscience, which contributed in the past to the abolition of slavery, and the creation of institutions ranging from trade unions and the Labour Party, to the Salvation Army and the *Manchester Guardian*.'

As the political debate in Britain increasingly centres on moral and social values, Walter Schwarz has talked to a cross-section of the upholders of today's Nonconformist Conscience. These 'new Dissenters' are to be found in the churches, in voluntary agencies, in social work, education, local government, academic life, and across the whole party political spectrum. Although differing on many issues, they are united in looking for practical and positive alternatives to the new consumerism, while continuing to work for social cohesion and justice.

The individuals whose ideas make up the core of this timely book include the Bishops of Durham and Liverpool, Eric Hobsbawm, Jonathon Porritt, Fran Bennett, Tim Brighouse, Usha Prashar, Tony Benn, Vernon Bogdanor, Hanif Kureishi, Jo Richardson and Bruce Kent.

Walter Schwarz is religious affairs correspondent of the *Guardian*, and author (with Dorothy Schwarz) of *Breaking Through: The Theory and Practice of Wholistic Living*.

Other titles in the **Society Today** series:

Martin Loney
Children Betrayed: The Politics of Child Abuse (October 1989)

Peter Newell
Children Are People Too: The Case Against Physical Punishment (July 1989)

Walter Schwarz
The New Dissenters: The Nonconformist Conscience in the Age of Thatcher (1989)

Colin Ward
Welcome Thinner City: Urban Survival in the Nineties (September 1989)

For further details, please write to the sales manager, Bedford Square Press, 26 Bedford Square, London WC1B 3HU.